TEACHING A CHILD TO TO PAY ATTENTION

Proverbs 4:20-27

by

Dr. Daniel R. Berger II

Teaching a Child to Pay Attention: Proverbs 4:20-27

Library of Congress Control Number: 2015901955

Trade Paperback ISBN: 978-0-9864114-2-7

Cover Artwork by: Elieser Loewenthal
Edited by: Laurie Buck

Published by Alethia International Publications

Taylors, SC - USA

drberger.dr@gmail.com

Printed in the United States of America.

To

my loving and faithful wife, Oriana

"He who finds a wife finds a good thing

and obtains favor from the LORD."

PROVERBS 18:22

TABLE OF CONTENTS

ABBREVIATIONS

APA   American Psychological Association

ADD   Attention Deficit Disorder

ADHD Attention Deficit Hyperactivity Disorder

DSM   *The Diagnostic and Statistical Manual of Mental Disorders IV*-TR

ESV   English Standard Version

KJV   King James Version

NASB New American Standard

NoSC *ADHD and the Nature of Self-Control*

TCoA *Taking Control of ADHD*

PREFACE

This book builds upon the foundation laid in *The Truth about ADHD: Genuine Hope and Biblical Help* (Taylors, SC: Alethia International Publications, 2014), which addresses the faulty secular paradigm that attempts to blame children's poor behavior and inability to pay attention on unproven biological inhibitors (not the receptive organs or validated brain damage). The book also exposes the foundational error in secularists' theories to be their faulty view of human nature, offers proven hope in Christ to deal with problems associated with the ADHD label, and answers pressing questions using the Word of God. This book differs from *The Truth about ADHD* in that it focuses on providing parents, teachers, and counselors with practical and biblical means to help teach and shape the attentional faculties of all children, especially those who struggle with behaviors represented in the secular paradigm of ADHD. This help is presented through the principles laid out in the book of Proverbs and specifically in Proverbs 4:20-27.

INTRODUCTION

Because paying attention is foundational to every relationship and fundamental to education, it is not surprising that Proverbs offers parents practical wisdom to help a child learn to rightly place his attention. Although Proverbs primarily speaks to the child's giving his attention to moral and practical wisdom,[1] learning and obedience to any instructions (including academic instructions) are achieved through these steps.[2]

---

[1] Regarding this type of wisdom, Waltke writes, "*To wisdom* (*lahokma*, see 1:2) refers to the substance of the parents' teaching—that is, the proverbs of Solomon. The aim of their education is not wisdom per se but as a vehicle for living (see 1:2; 2:20-22)" (Bruce K. Waltke, *The Book of Proverbs: Chapters 1-15*, New International Commentary on the Old Testament, ed. R. K. Harrison and Robert L. Hubbard Jr. [Grand Rapids: Eerdmans, 2004], 221).

[2] Proverbs 1:8 reads, "Hear, my son, your father's *instruction* [*musar*], and forsake not your mother's *teaching* [*tora*]." Children need to pay attention to their parents' instructions and directives whether moral, practical, academic, or otherwise (Derek Kidner, *Proverbs:* An Introduction and Commentary, vol. 15, Tyndale Old Testament Commentaries, ed. Donald J. Wiseman [Downers Grove: InterVarsity, 1975], 63).

A Difficult Endeavor

We must begin by realizing that this endeavor will not be easy —

paying attention is a difficult skill for all children to learn. To make this

matter more pressing, a child's failure to give attention rightly is to a

great degree responsible for his disobedience, incomplete work, poor

productivity, and over-all poor relationships. In his book *On Education,*

the philosopher Immanuel Kant wrote about this common human

struggle:

> With regard to the power of attention, we may remark that this
> faculty needs general strengthening. The power of rigidly
> fixing our thoughts upon one object is not so much a talent as a
> weakness of our mind, which in this case is inflexible, and does
> not allow itself to be applied at pleasure.[3]

This understanding — that giving someone else our attention rightly is a

normal struggle for all mankind — directly contradicts the unproven

ADHD construct. Before we can understand and define what is actually

abnormal we must first determine what is normal. In fact, research

findings continually show that the rates of children struggling to give

---

[3] Immanuel Kant, *On Education* (London: Kegan Paul, Trench, Trubner and Co., 1899), 79.

attention are much higher than once thought.[4] This reality along with extensive research have led renowned neuroscientist and psychiatrist Dr. Bruce Perry to conclude that attentional and behavioral struggles are common among us all. He states, "If you look at how you end up with [the ADHD] label, it is remarkable because any one of us at any given time would fit at least a couple of those criteria."[5] All children struggle to pay attention and not merely a small percentage of the population. Accepting this truth is foundational in understanding how to teach a child to pay attention, and we should therefore expect that the Word of God addresses man's natural bent and attentional problems.

Though the struggle to pay attention is common, no child manifests this problem in the same way. We must be careful that we do not fall prey to the same deception as secularists in thinking that behavior alone reveals the foundational problem. Though we can

---

[4] "Typical Toddler Behavior, or ADHD? 10 Ways to Tell"; available from http://www. livescience.com/22362-adhd-symptoms-guide.html; Internet.

[5] Daniel Boffey, "Children's hyperactivity 'is not a real disease', says US expert"; available from http://www.theguardian.com/society/2014/mar/30/children-hyperactivity-not-real-disease-neuroscientist-adhd; Internet.

certainly have insight into the hearts of children by their behavior, their behavior is not always an indication of the condition of their hearts before God. We are reminded in Scripture that man looks on the outward appearance, whereas God judges the heart. So while it might be convenient to identify children who struggle with giving attention by their maladaptive behavior (Proverbs 20:11), children who behave in a socially acceptable way still may have the same depraved attentional struggles. We must be careful not to make the child's behavior our primary concern or the chief aim of our discipline. Some things are for sure: all children are born with the need to pay attention rightly, and parents must make this need a priority as it is foundational to life.

A Clear Definition

While many in society today may view attention as a physical act accomplished by the eyes and ears, Scripture views learning to give one's attention as a moral exercise that includes the child's receptive senses, his inward faculties, and his volitional and complete obedience which ultimately make him successful and productive. When one speaks of getting a child's attention in a scriptural way, the child's engaged obedience/productivity also must be in view. For example, the commentator Tremper Longman III makes this observation: "The Hebrew word [*listen*] denotes more than the simple act of hearing; it implies obedience. The son must act on the instruction that follows, not just learn it as brute fact."[6] Another commentator also touches on this same idea in the wisdom literature: "To pay attention to a command entails carrying it out."[7] Giving attention rightly as Scripture sets forth, then, is the son using his natural senses to understand his parents' directives, internalizing them, and working hard to carry them out — it is not merely receiving information.

We must also realize, however, that even the secular paradigm of the ADHD construct — though its creators disagree with the biblical truth — also links attention and obedience. *The Diagnostic and Statistical Manual* (hereafter referred to as *DSM*),[8] which is the basis for ADHD

---

[6] Tremper Longman III, *Proverbs,* Baker Commentary on the Old Testament Wisdom and Psalms (Grand Rapids: Baker, 2006), 105.

[7] Waltke, *1-15,* 221.

[8] American Psychiatric Association, *Diagnostic and Statistical Manual of Mental Disorders: DSM-IV-TR* (Washington, D.C.: American Psychiatric Association, 2000). The

definitions and where the construct is born and thrives, lists three criteria under "hyperactivity," yet in actuality, these behaviors are disobedience. The first three criteria listed under "hyperactivity" in the *DSM* are "often gets up from his seat *when remaining in seat is expected* [emphasis added]," "often fidgets with hands or feet or squirms in seat *when sitting still is expected* [emphasis added]," and "often excessively runs about or climbs *when and where it is not appropriate* [emphasis added]."[9] In fact, the eighteen behaviors listed in the *DSM* as defining ADHD are all observable behaviors.

Worth also noting is the Chinese symbol "To Listen" which includes the ears, the eyes, the heart, and undivided attention.[10] The US government uses the symbol in training

Ears - to hear
Eyes - to see
Undivided attention to focus
Heart - to feel

聽心

American Psychiatric Association published a fifth revision of the *DSM* in May 2013. The changes to the new addition regarding ADHD were not significant, and the general premise of the ADHD label remains the same.

[9] *DSM*, 92.

[10] "Active Listening"; available from http://www.state.gov/m/a/os/65759.htm; Internet.

6

adolescents how to be active listeners and better manage stress. They state, "Active listening is a skill taught to teachers and police officers, counselors, ministers, rabbis and priests. It is a skill we would all do better having learned, practiced."[11] Though they may never admit it, secularists across many cultures and professions realize that a child's attention, the condition of his heart, and his behaviors are not separate.

Scripture does not focus primarily on behavior, but on the psychosomatic nature of the child that ultimately produces his behavior. Throughout the Bible the eyes, ears, heart/mind, and behavior are connected as one thought. This truth is repeated and thus emphasized in the book of Proverbs. In some passages the pattern is literal such as in Proverbs 4:20-27, while in other passages it is presented metaphorically using symbols such as in Deuteronomy 6:4-9. Throughout both the Old and New Testaments the pattern of attention is offered to explain rebellion, the deceptive nature of every man, the reality of lusts, the source of faith, and how one is morally educated (see chart A on the Biblical understanding of attention).

---

[11] Ibid.

7

CHART A – THE BIBLICAL UNDERSTANDING OF ATTENTION

Passages	The Receptive Organs		The Heart	The Behaviors
	The Ears	The Eyes		
Proverbs 4:20-27 & Repeated throughout Proverbs **Educationally (moral and otherwise)**	Stay attentive to wisdom Vs. 20	Stay focused on Wisdom Vs. 21	Keep in the heart Guard the heart Out of the heart come the issues of life Vs. 21 / 23	Mouth, eyes, feet Vs. 24-27
Deuteronomy 6:4-9 "The Shema" Deut. 11:18-21 **Symbolically**	Hear parental teaching Vs. 7	Bind them on your frontals/ write them on the doorframes /gates Vs. 8 / 9	Parent's heart becomes child's heart = *Values* Vs. 5-6 / 7	Tie them as symbols on your hands Vs. 8
Romans 11:8 Acts 28:27 Isaiah 6:9-10 Matt. 13:14-17 Deut. 29:4 **Morally**	Muted ears	Closed eyes	Calloused heart	
Ezekiel 12:2 John 8:43-47 **Naturally**	Do not hear	Do not see	Deceptive heart lacks understanding Rebellious	Deceptive mouth
Jeremiah 22:16-17 "to know me" **Relationally**	*declares* the Lord Vs. 16	Your eyes Vs. 17	Your Heart Intent only upon your own **dishonest gain"** = *Deceptive treasure* Vs. 17	Intent on shedding innocent blood … on practicing oppression and extortion Vs. 17
Job 31:1-7 **Specifically**		Covenant with eyes Vs. 1/7	If my heart followed my eyes If my heart has been enticed Vs. 7 / 9	Walked in falsehood Spot on hands Vs. 5 / 7

8

A Deficit in Attention?

For parents or teachers who are searching for answers in the face of an ADHD or ADD diagnosis, it is essential to note that the idea of a child's having a deficit in attention that impairs his ability to obey is mere speculation.[12] This type of child, in truth, is capable of giving attention;[13] even ADHD advocates admit that no deficit in attention actually exists.[14]

What does exist naturally in all children is the problem of misplaced attention. This point must be understood because it is emphasized throughout Proverbs as foundational to all types of education, direction in life, and ultimately the child's eternal destination. The reality that all children are born with their attention directed toward

---

[12] For further reading on the subject, see Daniel Berger, *The Truth about ADHD: Genuine Hope and Biblical Answers* (Taylors, SC: Alethia international Publications, 2014).

[13] This statement, of course, does not apply to children who have attentional problems across their entire life experience and not just in activities that lack interest to them. Valid physical impairments such as sensory impairments, autism, or brain damage can hinder a child's ability to give his attention. Many times children are incorrectly labelled as ADHD when they actually fall within the Autism spectrum.

[14] Russell A. Barkley, *ADHD and the Nature of Self-Control* (New York: Guilford, 2005), 79. Hereafter referred to as *NoSC*.

both their own opinion and toward vanity is evident even in children

labelled as having ADHD. They have the ability to direct their attention

at length toward things that please and interest them (such as video

games, sports, or movies) — which even secularists admit[15] — yet they

view education and parental instruction as having little value. In reality,

all children are born having misplaced attention and poor value systems;

therefore, the behaviors describing the secular construct of ADHD are

common among all children and even adults.[16] Children labelled as

ADHD are not abnormal, though they may struggle more than some to

find value in the wisdom of others. Secularists even admit that after

reading the criteria listed in the *DSM*, it would be easy to conclude that

everyone has ADHD.[17] Such a conclusion, though seemingly far-fetched,

is actually on point: everyone struggles in varying degrees with mental

---

[15] Katherine Ellison, "Brain Scans Link ADHD to Biological Flaw Tied to Motivation"; available from http://www.washingtonpost.com/wpdyn/content /article/2009/09/21/ AR2009092103100.html; Internet.

[16] Ibid.

[17] Enrico Gnaulati, *Back to Normal: Why Ordinary Childhood Behavior Is Mistaken for ADHD, Bipolar Disorder, and Autism Spectrum Disorder* (Boston: Beacon Press, 2013).

self-control, paying attention, behaviors, and so forth. Additionally, no objective standardized system of measurement exists to evaluate the degree of a child's misplaced attention. The chief way to discern what captures a child's attention is through careful observation of the child's behavior, though even this means of judgment can be misleading. As already referenced, passages such as Proverbs 20:11 and 14:24 Scripture declares that children (and adults) are judged by their behaviors.

So what is the answer to misplaced or misdirected attention? Fortunately, God's Word not only identifies the real problem, but also the solution. Proverbs 4:20-27 is one passage that records a pattern offered repeatedly throughout Proverbs and found throughout the Old Testament. Wise parents and teachers can utilize this pattern in teaching children to pay attention from an early age. In addition this pattern serves as the framework for this book. British commentator Derek Kidner titles this passage (4:20-27) "Concentrate," since he understands that the child needs "dogged attentiveness" in order to be productive.[18] Similarly, the commentator William McKane states that this passage is a

---

[18] *Proverbs*, 68.

"demand for attentiveness and retentiveness."[19] When believing parents

model and teach these steps and the child receives them, the child will

have the best opportunity to become successful in temporal and eternal

wisdom according to God's design. It is imperative to state again that

Proverbs intends the child to receive principally divine wisdom: the

highest of parental instructions. The principles, however, should be

applied to lesser educational and parental directives and help to teach

the child how, why, and on what to place his attention. This application

must be an urgent matter for parents and educators, since learning to

pay attention rightly is foundational to both the learner's temporal

success and his or her eternal destination.

A Distinction Made

Before we begin looking at Proverbs' steps to right attention, we

must first make a significant distinction between the universal human

struggle to focus and the valid physical impairments that limit the

ability to hear, see, and think. It is obvious that blindness, deafness, brain

---

[19] William McKane, *Proverbs: A New Approach* (Philadelphia: Westminster, 1970), 310.

injuries, autism, stress, lack of sleep, trauma, and other physical disorders can all affect a child's concentration, performance, and overall communication; therefore, a child with valid physical impairments will struggle to hear, see, think clearly, communicate, and remain focused in all of life's environments. Children who struggle with paying attention in all areas of life and not just when it is convenient, novel, or desirable should be evaluated by a physician for valid physical ailments/injuries. Yet, theorizing or trying to explain away a child's disobedience, antisocial behavior, and natural tendency to misplace his attention — such as the ADHD construct attempts to do — is an entirely different issue: disinclination is not disability. The failure to understand this subtle distinction has caused much unnecessary confusion and debate.

In addition, as parents consider the subjectivity and lack of proof surrounding the ADHD construct, they are sometimes confused by the notion that autism and ADHD are connected. Those who advocate such connections base them on problems of attention, which the *DSM* sets forth for both disorders. In fact, some doctors imply that the ADHD construct is a criterion for autism or that it is somehow connected, and

13

they even try to use EEG (electroencephalograph) results to tie the two

together. Brain scans and chemical testing, however, do not prove

ADHD, neither do they indicate connection with autism,[20] yet many

professionals speculate that they do and present this *post hoc* argument to

parents as scientifically undeniable.[21] EEGs do reveal neurological

problems, but the cause of those neurological variants cannot be

discerned by brain scans. Many studies suggest that a child's guilt,

shame, fear, and hurt are known to physically alter the anterior insula —

the region of the brain which oversees perception, emotion, and

relational interactions with other people.[22] Some even speculate that this

---

[20] "What to Do about the ADHD Epidemic," *American Academy of Pediatrics: Developmental and Behavioral Pediatrics Newsletter* (Autumn 2003): 6-7; available from http://www.ahrp.org/children/CareyADHD0603.php; Internet.

[21] *Post hoc ergo propter hoc* (after this therefore because this).

[22] ("Feelings of Guilt During Childhood Linked to Mental Illness"; available from http://www.huffingtonpost.com/2015/01/07/guilt-mental-health_n_6423434.html?cps=gravity_2692_-376788313446572831; Internet). One cannot conclude from neurological testing that the child's root cause of attentional problems is a physical or a spiritual problem. These tests merely reveal that there is a problem. If wrong thinking is to blame for brain atrophy or neurological variants, then the child's true problems are not physical at all and the neurological results are simply side-effects. "Anterior Insula Volume and Guilt: Neurobehavioral Markers of Recurrence after Early

neurological finding explains mental disorders such as ADHD. So the real problem is not even attention in these cases, but the cause of the child's guilt, shame, fear . . . . Other recent studies show that negative experiences or stresses — such as abuse, neglect, abandonment, and so forth — can negatively affect the physical brain structure and size leaving the child with neurological impairments:

> Neuroscientists have discovered how chronic stress and cortisol can damage the brain. A new study reconfirms the importance of maintaining healthy brain structure and connectivity by reducing chronic stress. Neuroscientists at the University of California, Berkeley, have found that chronic stress triggers long-term changes in brain structure and function. Their findings might explain why young people who are exposed to chronic stress early in life are prone to mental problems such as anxiety and mood disorders later in life, as well as learning difficulties . . . . "We studied only one part of the brain, the hippocampus, but our findings could provide insight into how white matter is changing in conditions such as schizophrenia, autism, depression, suicide, ADHD and PTSD," Kaufer said. The hippocampus regulates memory and emotions, and plays a role in various emotional disorders and has been known to shrink under extended periods of acute stress.[23]

Childhood Depressive Disorder"; available from http://archpsyc.jamanetwork.com/article.aspx?articleid=1935483; Internet.

[23] http://www.psychologytoday.com/blog/the-athletes-way/201402/chronic-stress-can-damage-brain-structure-and-connectivity; Internet.

There have even been claims that link a child's socioeconomic status with neurological dysfunction using EEG screening.[24] We must be careful that we do not take the findings of brain scans and apply a false theory of causation when none exists. What has become evident in recent neurological research is that many factors of a child's environment and experiences can alter his or her physical brain and neurological activity. However, these types of emotional or circumstantial impairments can also be reversed, and the brain can be restored to normal function.[25]

Neuroscientist Dr. Bruce Perry is convinced that if you can diminish or reverse the consequences of an adverse childhood experience, then what is commonly described as ADHD and much of the

---

[24] "EEGs show brain differences between poor and rich kids"; available from http://berkeley.edu/news/media/releases/2008/12/02_cortex.shtml; Internet.

[25] This reality is not suggesting that physical brain injuries or valid physical damage can always be reversed. Instead, the studies focused on how stress, trauma, and difficult life events can affect poorly the physical structure and spiritual mindsets of children. http://www.psychologytoday.com/blog/the-athletes-way/201402/chronic-stress-can-damage-brain-structure-and-connectivity; Internet.

cause of the child's dysfunction would be resolved. It is no wonder then, that he believes the ADHD label "is not a real disease."[26]

Additionally, most types of autism involve a child who is not connecting well with others around them and who struggles with giving attention in all situations of life because of objective physical impairments. These characteristics of most autistic children differ greatly from the alleged theories of ADHD. The *DSM*-V, however, opted not to give exclusions for ADHD when autism is present (if in fact ADHD were valid). Within the autism spectrum, it is widely understood that a child's attentional struggle and difficulty communicating impair his entire life, whereas in the ADHD construct, the child is allegedly impaired only when he finds no interest in a task, is not under close supervision, or is in

---

[26] Daniel Boffey, "Children's hyperactivity 'is not a real disease', says US expert"; available from http://www.theguardian.com/society/2014/mar/30/children-hyperactivity-not-real-disease-neuroscientist-adhd; Internet. Dr. Perry is not alone in his understanding that experiences shape the brain positively and negatively. Dr. Sharon Begley states in her book (which attempts to wed scientific findings with the teachings of the Dalai Lama), "By the middle of the twentieth century, then, neuroscientists had accumulated a compelling body of evidence that the brain is dynamic, remodeling itself continually in response to experience (Sharon Begley, *Train Your Mind Change Your Brain: How A New Science Reveals Our Extraordinary Potential to Transform Ourselves* [New York: Ballantine Books, 2008], 30)."

a familiar setting.[27] As a result, many refer to ADHD as an "interest deficit" and not an actual deficit in attention.[28] Many autistic children, due to their validated physical problems cannot give or maintain attention no matter how intense the supervision or how interesting an activity might be. Furthermore, autism is known to be partly a sensory impairment disorder — the disorder negatively affects the eyes and ears, which are the receptive organs.[29] With ADHD, there is no proven physical impairment of the senses. In truth, these two ideas — one a valid disease (autism) and the other a subjective construct (ADHD) — cannot coexist by the *DSM*'s own definitions. This reality has raised much controversy and dialogue even among professionals:

> According to the DSM-IV-TR, symptoms of inattention and hyperactivity are frequent in children with Autism Spectrum Disorders (ASD). This statement is supported by clinical

---

[27] *DSM-IV*, 86-87.

[28] Katherine Ellison, "Brain Scans Link ADHD to Biological Flaw Tied to Motivation"; available from http://www.washingtonpost.com/wpdyn/content/article/2009/09/21/ AR2009092103100.html; Internet. Russell A. Barkley, *ADHD and the Nature of Self-Control* (New York: Guilford, 2005), 79. Hereafter referred to as *NoSC*

[29] "The Sensory World of Autism"; available from http://www.autism.org.uk/sensory; Internet.

observation and formal assessment. However, ASD diagnosis is still among the exclusion criteria for the Attention-Deficit/Hyperactivity Disorder (ADHD). Such exclusion generates controversy and questions regarding the need and benefits of maintaining or not these separations; so much so, that the proposed criteria for the DSM-V eliminate that exclusion condition.[30]

DSM committees should have recognized this error in their theories and corrected it, yet no exclusion exists in the fifth revision. The validated impairment that comes within the autism spectrum rightly explains the child's attentional problems, and the ADHD construct adds no value to understanding the child.

To make matters worse, the attempt to tie these two disorders together actually goes against the *DSM*'s own requirements for diagnosing ADHD: they must not be mistaken for other disorders that are environmentally caused or meet similar criteria.[31] If a child's senses are impaired (he has "sensory integration difficulties"), then by the *DSM*'s own definitions, the ADHD construct should not apply to the child. This *DSM* criteria is why author Dr. Richard Saul believes that

[30] "Attention-Deficit/Hyperactivity Disorder in Autism Spectrum Disorders"; available from http://www.ncbi.nlm.nih.gov/pubmed/21866791; Internet.

[31] *DSM-IV*, 90-93. *DSM-V* states the same.

ADHD does not exist and instead he attributes attentional behaviors to other conditions.[32] In reality, attaching a subjective construct to an objective brain disease not only adds confusion and hurt, but it can even make matters worse. Though many doctors still attempt to connect the two, we must understand and establish this clear distinction. If noticeable impairments exist in a child's ability to be attentive in all the settings of his or her life, or if he or she has trouble communicating, then a physician should evaluate the child for valid physical impairments or damage.

A Responsibility Established

One of the most important elements in the discussion of attention is that of responsibility. Both Proverbs and all of Scripture present three participants in moral education and the child's giving attention rightly: they are the child himself, the parent or instructor, and the Holy Spirit.

---

[32] Richard Saul, *ADHD Does Not Exist: The Truth about Attention Deficit and Hyperactivity Disorder* (New York: HarperCollins, 2014), 14.

Though Proverbs has all children in mind,[33] the child in

Proverbs whom the father addresses is a gullible male child most likely

on the brink of manhood for whom "a decision to join the wise is

imperative in order to have the sage's knowledge."[34] Within the

historical context of Proverbs, the father's address to his older child was

not his first time teaching his son divine wisdom. It should be assumed

this was a common practice throughout the son's life, since in the first

nine chapters of the book of Proverbs, the father repeats ten times the

directive to pay attention. Furthermore, in Jewish culture intense

teaching began at an early age:

> The father began the stern teaching soon after the child had
> been weaned, to judge from the example of Samuel (cf.
> Proverbs 20:11; 22:6). As soon as Hannah had weaned Samuel,
> she brought him to the temple at Shiloh, where the high priest

---

[33] Murphy states the intended audience of Proverbs and the universal implications. He writes, "It should be emphasized that 'my son' is not to be taken in a gender exclusive sense. This book is for all Israel, and the observations deal with universal human experience, except in very few cases" (Rowland E. Murphy, *Proverbs*, vol. 22 of Word Biblical Commentary [Dallas: Word, 1998], 12).

[34] Ibid., 178. Waltke concludes that Proverbs 4:3 indicates that the child was very young, inexperienced, and completely dependent upon his father and mother when his education began.[34] (277-78).

Eli immediately began Samuel's tutelage (cf. 1 Sam 1). In the ancient Near East weaning happened after three years of age.[35]

Therefore, it is logical to assume then that the wisdom presented in Proverbs was not withheld from the son prior to his moving toward maturity, but was taught to him by Solomon from the earliest of years, just as Solomon had learned from his father.[36] The key here is that the parent is consistently and purposefully teaching the child to walk wisely and ultimately to embrace the parent's teaching as his own. However, because each child is different and learns and understands at a different rate, parents must discern the child's capabilities and approach him accordingly.

> Of course we must be wise and age-appropriate. We must not hold a child responsible for what is impossible for their stage of growth (i.e., a ten-month-old probably is not ready to make his bed or empty the trash). At the same time, many parents expect far too little of their children, and thus end up with immature youth. Think of this particularly in terms of obedience. We should start expecting our child to respect and obey us from the earliest reasonable days. I have observed for many years that far too many parents simply do not expect to

---

[35] Ibid.,

[36] Kidner, *Proverbs*, 51, 105.

22

be obeyed. If a child can obey, then he should be required to obey.[37]

Still, wise parenting will not guarantee that children will internalize their parents' teaching. Proverbs 22:6 is not a promise that if parents discipline their children correctly they will turn out ok. Instead, it establishes the parents as responsible to choose the target and course of arrival for the child's life. In so many words, the verse states: If you want your child to be something, you must dedicate and direct him in this way.

It is clear in Scripture that parents have a responsibility to both dedicate their child in the way that he should go as well as to actively oversee his journey towards that goal. This responsibility pertains to both the highest moral directives and to simple daily tasks. Though parents are responsible to discipline their children toward Christ (wisdom), there are other key participants who likewise bear responsibility.

---

[37] Dan Phillips, *God's Wisdom in Proverbs: Hearing God's Voice in Scripture* (The Woodlands, Tex.: Kress Biblical Resources, 2011), 283.

In Proverbs, the father places his son in a position of responsibility for hearing and seeing, treasuring his imperatives, guarding his own heart, accepting, and purposefully carrying out the instructions. So, obviously, the child also plays a role in the outcome of his life and will answer to God for the same. The meaning of *understanding* presented repeatedly through Proverbs reveals an idea of being in between something or faced with two choices as at a fork in the road. The child must receive and carryout his father's instruction or refuse correction and wisdom and continue to trust in his own way as fools naturally do (Proverbs 28:16). Whether in moral education or academic learning, both instructor and student have responsibilities in order to achieve established and agreed-upon outcomes.

In moral education, however, the third participant is the Holy Spirit. His role is significant, as without his involvement, no understanding can even occur. First Corinthians 2:4-16 reveals that it is only through the work of the Holy Spirit that understanding of divine wisdom is achieved. Likewise, Proverbs 2:6 clearly indicates that it is the

Lord himself who gives knowledge and understanding: "For the LORD gives wisdom; from his mouth come knowledge and understanding."[38]

These three participants are relevant to our discussion on attention, not only because all must fulfill their responsibility, but also they must realize that they are incapable of fulfilling the others' responsibilities. Many parents get frustrated and even blame themselves for their children's choices when they have pursued the Lord with all their heart and taught their child as best they could (Proverbs 2:1). Yet the child must himself value and desire God, he must cry out for the Lord to save him (Proverbs 2:2-5), and he must accept lady wisdom's invitation to enter into a covenant with her (Proverbs 8). Likewise, the Lord must give understanding unto wisdom. Unless parents reject or rebel against divine wisdom, they should not look at the outcome of their child's moral education or any point in between and judge themselves accordingly. Some parents, however, see God's work in their children's lives as evidence of their own achievement, whereas others question what they could have done differently to produce a better

---

[38] The *ESV* will be used throughout this book unless otherwise noted.

outcome in the life of a child. Neither of these mindsets are healthy thinking: salvation and sanctification are the complete work of the Holy Spirit, and God even uses non-Christians and disobedient believers — such as the prophet Jonah was to the Ninevites — to reveal his wisdom and provide understanding. What must be present in the parent's own lives is a personal and intimate relationship with God that sets as their own goal to know and please the Lord. Having this personal discipline centered upon the Word of God will dedicate and motivate the child to pursue the same (Deut. 6:4-9; Proverbs 23:26; see appendix A). Though children may not appear to be paying attention, parents still have a responsibility to diligently and wisely discipline their children toward right goals. Such discipline requires patience, focus on future reward, trust in the Lord, and complete dependence on God for right results.

STEP 1 – TRAIN THE RECEPTIVE ORGANS (20-21A)

For a child to offer his attention correctly, he must first be taught

how to control his eyes and ears. These organs are the learner's chief

physical instruments with which he gives attention and by which

education occurs.[39] Proverbs 4:20-21 says, "My son, be attentive to my

words; incline your ear to my sayings. Let them not escape from your

sight; keep them within your heart" (20-21). Waltke writes of this

passage, "Logically, the introduction [to this section in Proverbs 4]

mentions the receptive organs (ears, 20), eyes (21a), and heart

(21b, 23a)."[40] As with the rest of the body, the eyes, ears, and mind need

exercise and ordered experiences to form right habits and ideas and to

learn self-control. The whole body must learn to work together in order

---

[39] As previously noted, damaged or physically impaired eyes or ears will make
giving attention difficult for the child, and a physician should check both (Julian Stuart
Haber, *ADHD: The Great Misdiagnosis* [New York: Taylor Trade, 2003], 47-48). Also for
children without valid physical disabilities, spanking stimulates the senses as needed to
gain the child's attention and help him to respond correctly to instructions.

[40] Bruce K. Waltke, *The Book of Proverbs: Chapters 1-15*, New International
Commentary on the Old Testament, ed. R. K. Harrison and Robert L. Hubbard Jr. (Grand
Rapids: Eerdmans, 2004), 296.

27

to live successfully. Though their verbal instructions are clearly important and even faith comes from hearing (Romans 10:17), parents must consider the practical wisdom gained by the child through physical repetition and the experience of the child controlling his own mind and body.

God's design of the eyes and ears to receive and shape the heart is significant (Proverbs 20:12). In fact, modern neuroscience reveals that the connection between the mind/heart and the senses is more powerful than once imagined. Renowned neuroscientist Vilayanur Ramachandran has done groundbreaking work which among other things has shown how the physical brain, the immaterial mind, and the body — specifically the eyes — work together.[41] Additionally, he scientifically expounds (unintentionally of course) on how deceptive the mind can be — a point which Scripture sets forth as vital to understanding the natural condition of everyone's heart (Jeremiah 17:9). One illustration that he presents is that of phantom pains, which amputees often experience. Prior to the

---

[41] "VS Ramachandran: The Marco Polo of Neuroscience"; available from http://www.theguardian.com/theobserver/2011/jan/30/observer-profile-vs-ramachandran; Internet.

amputation of their damaged limb, these patients experience severe pain in the damaged appendage. Desiring to eliminate the pain, they plead with their doctors to amputate. After the surgery, however, the pain persists even without the patient's limb present. This common experience has led many neurologists to theorize that much of our supposed physical pain is actually mere mental perception or habituation rather than the result of tangible physical causes. So intense and persistent is the phantom pain of some of these individuals that many of them commit suicide in an attempt to deliver themselves from their suffering. In these cases, part of the body was absent, yet the mind had learned its pain prior to the amputation and would not think differently or realistically. The mind was deceived and trained, even though the patient was aware that the limb was not still attached.

To treat this phenomenon, Dr. Ramachandran developed a method to relieve and even eliminate the pain in the phantom limb — focusing on the patient's eyes. His treatment requires patients to place their good limb in front of a mirror, which makes it appear as though the amputated limb is still whole and healthy. Patients then move the healthy limb according to their wishes, and the eyes and brain see this mirroring as their ability to control the phantom limb. Dr. Ramachandran notes that these individuals are not crazy — they are well aware of what is taking place. Yet the visual stimulation, in spite of knowing the reality, retrains the mind to think differently about the circumstances. Over time, through this visual stimulation and habituation, patients begin to recover.

Not only do such studies reveal the deceptive nature of our natural hearts,[42] they also expose the power of physical sight in every aspect of life. God has designed the eyes to engage the brain in order to shape the patient's mind and help him to think truthfully (see Appendix B). This illustration also explains why faith goes against the nature of who we are, since faith is not based on what we see but on what we hear (Romans 10:17) and believe to be true (Hebrews 11:1-3). It is no wonder, then, that Proverbs speaks often of the connection between the heart and the body — specifically, the receptive organs which are the eyes and ears

---

[42] Jeremiah 17:9 states that "the heart is deceitful above all things and desperately sick." Our hearts are very good at deceiving us, and truth and right thinking are foundational to our restoration and remedy.

(Proverbs 4:20-27). God designed the body and mind/heart not to be separate entities but to work together, and parents must not neglect to help their children train their bodies.

When the eyes are given to something repeatedly, this habituation shapes the mind. Video games, pornography, advertisements, images of what a young lady should physically look like in magazines, and TV programs to name a few constantly influence the mind's thinking. Likewise, positive examples and parents' own lifestyles impact the child's mind through repeated observation (Proverbs 23:26), and study is based upon this truth. When it comes to all realms of learning, the applications of this reality are staggering.

By teaching their children to control their physical bodies, parents begin teaching them to give honor to others — to favor someone above themselves, an action which goes against their natural mindset. In Ephesians 6:1-3, children are commanded to honor or favor their parents above themselves and to obey. Parents first can teach the child to honor them by physically training the eyes because "'to set the eyes' on anyone is to view him with favour (Gen. 44:21; Job 24:23; Jer. 39:12)."[43] If children are to favor their parents' instructions above their own thinking, they must be taught to do so.[44] This behavior will most likely not occur if a child is left to his own natural way. The example of God the Father allows us to see how important this concept is in parenting: God himself sets his favor or grace[45] on those who set their eyes on him and other people, and he opposes[46] those whose eyes are focused on themselves (i.e., they favor themselves above others or are proud; 1 Peter 5:5).[47]

---

[43] M. G. Easton, *Easton's Bible Dictionary* (New York: Harper, 1893).

[44] Tedd Tripp, *Shepherding a Child's Heart* (Wapwallopen, Pa.: Shepherd Press, 1995), 136.

[45] "*Grace* is God's undeserved favour toward us, and is needed not only to save us from eternal judgment but also to enable us to live the Christian life" (Wayne A. Grudem, *1 Peter: An Introduction and Commentary*, vol. 17 of Tyndale New Testament Commentaries [Downers Grove: InterVarsity, 1988], 200); see also J. Ramsey Michaels, *1 Peter*, vol. 49 of Word Biblical Commentary (Dallas: Word, 1998), 290.

[46] Proverbs 3:34 is often cited as the basis for Peter's writing: "Toward the scorners he is scornful, but to the humble he gives favor" (ibid., 200); see also Kidner, *Proverbs*, 66.

[47] "They assault, as it were, the honor of God in seizing that which belongs to God" (John Peter Lange, et al., *A Commentary on the Holy Scriptures: 1 Peter* [Bellingham, Wash.: Logos Bible Software, 2008], 89). Proverbs 3:7 states the same idea: "Be not wise in your own eyes; fear the Lord, and turn away from evil" (Cohen, 14; Kidner, *Proverbs*, 64).

Since giving attention to someone else's inclinations is contrary to a child's natural way of thinking but vital to the educational process, parents must train their children to pay attention and to understand why paying attention is essential.

This teaching should begin with training the physical eyes to properly give attention. If one cannot physically focus his attention or control his eyes, then he cannot guard his heart, and this lack of self-control will be seen in the rest of his body. The focus of the eyes not only reflects the focus of the heart (its desires),[48] but it teaches the heart.[49] For example, Matthew 5:28 states, "But I say to you that everyone who looks at a woman with lustful intent has already committed adultery with her in his heart." God forbids man to use his body to fulfill his lusts, and

---

[48] "Singleness of purpose is one great secret of spiritual prosperity. If our eyes do not see clearly we cannot walk without stumbling and falling. If we attempt to work for two different masters, we are sure to give satisfaction to neither. It is just the same with respect to our souls. We cannot serve Christ and the world at the same time: it is vain to attempt it. The thing cannot be done: the ark and Dagon will never stand together (see 1 Samuel 5). God must be king over our hearts: his law, his will, his precepts must receive our first attention; then, and not till then, everything in our inner being will fall into its right place. Unless our hearts are set in order like this, everything will be in confusion. 'Your whole body will be full of darkness' (verse 23)" (Ryle, 43). See also Waltke, 1-15, 92.

[49] Waltke, 1-15, 296.

33

man's obedience must start with his eyes. Matthew 6:22-23 says, "The eye is the lamp of the body. So, if your eye is healthy, your whole body will be full of light, but if your eye is bad, your whole body will be full of darkness. If then the light in you is darkness, how great is the darkness!" In the spiritual sense, if one cannot give his attention singularly (that is, have "one eye" or one fixed pursuit), then he wanders without singular direction, and his body will follow.[50] Proverbs lists the receptive organs — the eyes, the ears, and the heart — together, since they typically coordinate to receive and store information.[51] It is no wonder, then, that a man like Job made a "covenant with [his] eyes" (Job 31:1) that he would not look at a woman to lust after her. He realized that if he did not control his physical eyes, then not only his heart, but the rest of his

---

[50] "The result of such a *sound eye* is a well-illuminated *body*. The body here represents the whole person, and if the idea of the lamp was of that which enables the body to find its way, the thought is of a purposeful life, directed towards its true goal. The alternative is a life in the dark, like a blind man, because the 'evil eye' of selfish materialism gives no light to show the way" (R. T. France, *Matthew: An Introduction and Commentary*, vol. 1 of Tyndale New Testament Commentaries [Downers Grove: InterVarsity, 1985], 143).

[51] Waltke, *1-15*, 296.

body would follow.[52] The next several verses show that his decision was based upon his spiritual eyes (heart's desire and pursuit). In verse 5 Job mentions his feet that would follow: "If I have walked with falsehood and my foot has hastened to deceit." He goes on in verse 7 to make it clear that the heart follows what the eyes entertain: "If my step has turned aside from the way and *my heart has gone after my eyes* [emphasis added], and if any spot has stuck to my hands, then let me sow, and another eat . . . ." Similarly, if a child is allowed to pursue and have all that his eyes (heart) desire, then he learns this way of life and behaves accordingly. Learning to control one's physical eyes helps to guard the heart against the natural way of thinking (the lust of the eyes/flesh) and eventually from evil influences, which can encourage wrong desires and

---

[52] Proverbs often connects the eyes and feet in showing one's direction on the way (i.e., lifestyle; 4:25-26). Other Old Testament passages also connect the eyes and the hand (as in Deut. 6:8, "You shall bind them as a sign on your hand, and they shall be as frontlets between your eyes."). The receptive organs (eyes in this verse) are once again connected with its active members (hands) (Waltke, *1-15*, 296).

lead to wrong actions. Thus, a person goes where he is looking, so to speak.[53]

To train their child's eyes, parents will need to take a hands-on approach. Besides verbally instructing the child to look him in the eyes, a parent can gently turn the young child's face toward his own in order to establish eye contact and show the child what is required in giving attention. Most children will not like giving their attention in this way, and many will immediately look away. In doing so, they reveal the natural bent of their hearts. Parents may also need to turn off electronic devices, take the child into a quiet room, or eliminate other distractions in order to properly gain their attention. Yelling commands across the house or up the stairs, however, is not a good way to teach bodily control or acceptable communication.

---

[53] It is worth noting in the discussion on the eyes, that the child's observation of his parent's own pursuits and lifestyle also discipline the child. In Proverbs 23:26 the Father says to his son: "My son, give me your heart, and let your eyes observe my ways." Consistent close observation of parents' behavior teaches the authenticity of the parents' faith and can either motivate the child toward or dissuade him from embracing the wisdom of God.

STEP 2 – FOCUS ON THE HEART (21B-24)

When the ears and eyes are engaged, parents must then focus on reaching the child's heart with their instructions. McKane comments on Proverbs 21, "It is in the mind (*leb*) that teaching is retained, revitalized and so assimilated that it belongs to a man as his inalienable possession."[54] Reaching the heart/mind involves addressing the child's understanding, his emotions, his desires, his motives, his natural bent, his goals, and his own sense of responsibility (see illustration A). Like a husband who answers his wife while watching a game without truly understanding what she is communicating or possibly his own response, so it is common for children to hear instructions without internalizing them. It is imperative, though, for the child to give his attention rightly to his parents by not only accepting information, but also learning to retain, value it, and guard it in his heart. Verse 21b instructs the child to "keep [the words] within [his] heart." Properly giving attention requires the eyes, the ears, and the heart all to be engaged.

---

[54] McKane, 310.

GETTING ATTENTION RIGHTLY

- Pray for biblical change

- Engage the eyes and ears

- Aim for understanding

- Confront the natural foolishness

- Encourage right responses

- Teach right motives & desires/ treasures

- Provide plans to arrive at goals

- Form beneficial habits

- Diligently supervise

- Emphasize personal responsibility

- Warn of besetting distractions

The child's heart

Aim for Understanding

In order for instructions to reach the mind, the child must first understand them. Though obvious, this fact is easily overlooked. Proverbs teaches that a hearer cannot receive divine wisdom or parental instruction without understanding.[55] Therefore, parents must strive for their children's understanding and expect their children to receive their instructions only as the instructions are age appropriate and in accordance with the child's ability to comprehend information.[56] As children grasp instructions and obey them, they learn through "exercise

---

[55] Boice also notes that in "God's school" understanding is essential to learning and obedience (990-91).

[56] Understanding of divine wisdom comes only through the work of the Holy Spirit. In fact, Scripture once again uses the metaphor of the eyes to illustrate man's lack of understanding in his heart. The eyes and the heart are very much connected. John 12:40 states, "He has blinded their eyes and hardened their heart, lest they see with their eyes, and understand with their heart, and turn, and I would heal them" (William Hendriksen and Simon J. Kistemaker, *Exposition of the Gospel According to John*, vol. 2 of New Testament Commentary [Grand Rapids: Baker, 2012], 212). Parents, however, must exercise common sense and discernment in choosing which aspects of practical wisdom to teach their children. It is not necessary to teach every application of wisdom to a young child who not only is incapable of understanding some aspects of wisdom, but also who does not yet need to apply that truth to his life. For example, parents should teach a five-year-old boy the importance of listening to his father's instructions in order to please the Lord and the value of remembering God's wisdom. He can also benefit from understanding how the ant fulfills its responsibilities without an authority standing over it. Parents should wait for the appropriate time, however, to teach the same young man the dangers of drunkenness or the strange woman.

of study" to embrace truth.[57] Understanding is key because obedience

and wisdom cannot take root and grow without it. Furthermore, it gives

the child an opportunity to behave obediently and appropriately.[58]

Demanding obedience without clear instructions is not only foolish, it is

confusing and hurtful.

So important are these truths that Proverbs begins by speaking

about the issue of understanding. Proverbs 1:1-6 presents: (1) words of

understanding — representing the instruction/instructor [v. 2], (2) the

one who is able to receive understanding — the student [v. 5], (3) and the

goal of the moral teaching – understanding which in moral education is

salvation [v. 6-7]. Even in temporal education, understanding is clearly a

goal that good teachers pursue and eager students possess. When it

comes to moral education, we must be diligent to fulfill our

---

[57] Waltke, *1-15*, 177.

[58] In Proverbs, to possess moral understanding is to live an ordered life: "In this book perceptive and competent people have insight into the moral order and social conscience that mold their activity. They have a cool spirit (i.e., self-control; 17:27), are patient (14:29), hold their tongues (11:29), can plumb the depths of another's heart (20:5), and keep a straight course (15:21). Fools find no delight in this moral imperative (18:2), and tyrants lack it (28:16)" (Waltke, *1-15*, 96-97).

responsibility and careful to depend upon God to bring about the goal of wisdom.

All education, whether moral or temporal, requires the student to diligently exercise his mind in order to gain understanding. Kant keenly observed that "everything in education depends upon establishing correct principles, and leading children to understand and accept them."[59] For the child who does not listen, lacks control over his eyes, is hyperactive, and is careless in considering his ways, understanding parental instructions (education) can seem impossible. Parents and teachers must keep in mind that "since wisdom comes from carefully considering our ways and listening to the wise, it can be a greater challenge for those who are naturally more active and less reflective."[60] Still, though some children do require more diligent effort and work than others, all children need to exercise their minds and form right habits. Scientific research has even shown that the brain itself is

---

[59] Kant, 108.

[60] Edward T. Welch, *A.D.D. Wandering Minds and Wired Bodies* (Phillipsburg, N.J.: Presbyterian and Reformed, 1999), 12.

much more pliable than once thought—circumstances and mindsets are now shown to affect the physical size and growth of the brain, much like any muscle in the body needs proper exercise.[61] The brain is so pliable and resilient, that through repetition, it is now known that the brain can sometimes transfer functions of a damaged area to healthy regions of the brain and reorganize its sensory map.[62] Even in the face of valid physical impairments and brain injuries, people have been known to regain full mental capacity when repetition and compassion are in place.[63] Secularists such as Dr. Jeffrey Schwartz and Dr. Rebecca Gladding have written books on "self-directed neuroplasticity," which they describe as eliminating bad brain habits through mental repetition and suggest that

---

[61] http://www.psychologytoday.com/blog/the-athletes-way/201402/chronic-stress-can-damage-brain-structure-and-connectivity; Internet.

[62] This adaptability of the brain is commonly known as neuroplasticity or cortical remapping. "Neuroplasticity: You can Teach an Old Brain New Tricks" available from http://bigthink.com/think-tank/brain-exercise; Internet. See also "Brain Plasticity?"; available from http://psychology.about.com /od/biopsychology/f/brain-plasticity.htm; Internet.

[63] Dr. Jeffrey Schwartz and Dr. Rebecca Gladding, *You Are Not Your Brain: The 4-Step Solution for Changing Bad Habits, Ending Unhealthy Thinking, and Taking Control of Your Life* (New York: Penguin Group, 2012).

such exercises form "a basis for hope and motivation."[64] The process of such habituation (whether self-imposed or under another's care) is often referred to as therapy. Whereas modern neuroscientists and physicians may suggest that they have discovered new techniques that can physically alter the brain in a positive way, mental exercise has existed as a key component to make the physical brain and the non-physical mind strong. Still, apart from God's wisdom, the heart and mind are incurably sick and no remedy exists other than the grace of God to restore man to full mental health. Proverbs 4:22 insists that inclining one's ear to wisdom and retaining it, provides the receiver with life and physical health.[65]

Repeat Instructions

Since understanding comes through mental exercise, parents need to exercise their child's mind, and one way do so is to repeat important directives. The natural tendency of people and especially

---

[64] Ibid., 82-88.

[65] Waltke, *1-15*, 297.

youth is to be forgetful,[66] so until a child can learn to meditate for himself, he must be taught how to do so. The book of Proverbs demonstrates the necessity of repetition in inculcating wisdom, as it begins the first nine chapters with the father's exhortation for his son to give him his attention. Kidner writes, "The constant repetition of such a call (introducing nearly every paragraph of this section of the book) is deliberate, for a major part of godliness lies in dogged attentiveness to familiar truths."[67] This lesson requires that parents repeat instructions often and in a variety of ways in order to clarify expectations as well as to emphasize their importance.

Additionally, parents can exercise the child's mind by asking the child questions about their instructions or requiring them to verbally repeat directives in their own words. Doing this exercise not only allows the child to think through the directives himself and engrain them into his mind, but it also provides parents the opportunity to see if the child

---

[66] Christensen states, "The human condition is to forget" (*Deuteronomy 1–21:9*, vol. 6A of Word Biblical Commentary [Dallas: Word, 2001], 174).

[67] Kidner, *Proverbs*, 68.

understands their instructions; they can know what is stored in the child's heart by what comes out of his or her mouth (Luke 6:45).

The child speaking the commands and repeating the parents' expectations, both solidifies them for the child and communicates to his parents whether their instructions have reached the heart.[68] In fact, secularists acknowledge the importance of children verbalizing their thoughts: "The most successful students learn to quietly verbalize what they think, and they use these verbalizations to guide their academic and social behaviors."[69] David exemplifies this pattern. He says in Psalm 119:13, "With my lips I declare all the rules of your mouth." If children cannot verbalize parents' communication to them, then parents need to repeat them until they are assured that their directives are stored in the child's heart. Repetition is key to right attention, education, and ultimately to godly character.[70] According to Jewish rabbis, "One who

---

[68] Waltke, *1-15*, 299.

[69] Richard L. Curwin, Allen N. Mendler and Brian D. Mendler, *Discipline With Dignity: New Challenges, New Solutions*, 3rd ed. (Alexandria, Va.: Association for Supervision and Curriculum Development, 2008), 149.

[70] Kidner, *Proverbs*, 68.

repeats his lessons a hundred times is not like one who repeats it a hundred and one times!"[71] Similarly, it has been said in academic education that unless a student can repeatedly verbalize or even teach his subject, then he has not yet fully learned.

But just how powerful is repetition in shaping attention and ultimately the mind and heart? One of the classic illustrations that sheds light on this topic is that of Polish psychologist Dr. Laszlo Polgar.[72] He first theorized that parents or any instructor could make a genius out of a child by diligently engaging them in repetitive behavior. He speculated that if a child began an activity at an early age and repeated that same activity over 10,000 hours in their lifetime, they would become a master of the same. But his theory became an experiment when he subjected his three daughters to the discipline of chess, which boasted less than 1 percent of grand masters to be women.[73] Not only were the girls

---

[71] C.f. Waltke, *1-15*, 220.

[72] "The Grandmaster Experiment"; available from http://www.psychologytoday.com /articles/200506/the-grandmaster-experiment; Internet.

[73] Ibid.

homeschooled, but they were also taught to play chess from an early age with structured and deliberate training. The result, the girls became not only grand masters, but some of the highest ranking chess players in history.

Obviously repeating verbal instruction is vital in teaching a child to pay attention and then to internalize parental wisdom, but the importance of repetition extends to nonverbal parental behavior as well. Parents must be purposeful in creating consistent home routines where the same actions are performed in a predictable way at a predictable time. Such routines are, of course, an exercise in repetition. This type of environment teaches children how to conduct themselves in an orderly way, and it also builds trust in the parents as knowable and dependable authority figures. In addition, children excel and even find security in the structure that is created. This reality is also seen in many children with valid physical impairments, such as autism, that hinder their ability to concentrate and communicate. Structure usually is the friend of learning. Whether verbal repetition or physical habits, repetition with right motivation is a key biblical component to right attention and education. It is no wonder then, that the father in Proverbs repeats to his son ten times in the first nine chapters the call to give him his attention — it was clearly important that his son treasures his words and obey.

As parents train their child to repeat important information and discipline the mind, they ultimately teach the child to do this exercise for himself. Scripture refers to the volitional discipline of one's own mind in mental repetition for his own benefit as *meditation*. It is through repetition that an idea or truth is memorized and becomes part of the character.[74] Secularists sometimes use the term "self-verbalization" to describe some of the same ideas involved in scriptural meditation:

> Self-verbalizing typically involves teaching the student to ask questions of himself about the nature of the problem, give himself instructions about the performance of the task, and provide appropriate reinforcement and corrective feedback. Lots of practice is often necessary for this skill to become internalized."[75]

---

[74] "Memorizing is precisely what is called for, since it is only when the Word of God is readily available in our minds that we are able to recall it in moments of need and profit by it" (Boice, 978). Similarly, Alden writes, "The sound counsel of godly parents is one kind of advice that ought to be memorized" (47). Kant also states, "Memory depends upon our attention" (79).

[75] Curwin et al., 149-50.

Meditation or "self-verbalizing" is not practiced merely to retain information or make it a part of the heart; ultimately it is done in order to carry out a task, to obey, or to be successful. Joshua 1:8 states,

> This Book of the Law shall not depart from your mouth, but you shall meditate on it day and night, so that you may be careful to do according to all that is written in it. For then you will make your way prosperous, and then you will have good success.

Likewise David states his purpose for meditation in Psalm 119:11: "I have stored up your word in my heart that I might not sin against you."[76] To progress in holiness and to obey God require that meditation and ultimately memorization be a constant exercise. True education must reach the heart, and repetition, meditation, and memorization are key exercises in learning to pay attention in such a way that obedience, prosperity and success can be realized by the child.

Encourage Right Responses

Additionally, parents and teachers can encourage their children by rejoicing in their obedience. In Proverbs 4:13, the father considers it a

---

[76] Kidner remarks, "Proverbs 2:10–12 and Colossians 3:16 show that the mind which stores up Scripture has its taste and judgment educated by God" (ibid., 459).

priority to encourage his son to continue diligently in his discipline.[77]

When the task is complete, encouragement is likewise beneficial.

Proverbs 10:1 states, "A wise son makes a glad father, but a foolish son is

a sorrow to his mother."[78] Parents' loving encouragement engages the

child's emotions (an important part of his heart)[79] and motivates the

child to progress in obedience and to complete set objectives.[80] Fremont

writes, "A compassionate teacher uses positive reinforcement to build

the [child's] confidence in succeeding at learning."[81] This encouragement

not only provides an emotional affirmation, but prods the heart to future

---

[77] The father was not giving the son new instructions, but encouraging his son to continue and to endure (Jay Adams, *The Christian Counselor's Commentary: Proverbs* [Woodruff, S.C.: Timeless Texts, 1997], 40). Likewise, Longman notes that the son is already obeying his father's instructions, but he is encouraged by the father to continue to do so (152).

[78] Kidner, *Proverbs*, 84.

[79] Kidner notes that Proverbs 15:15 and 30 reveal that the heart includes the emotions (*Proverbs*, 68).

[80] Boice, 994; Adams, *CCC Proverbs*, 71.

[81] Walter and Trudy Fremont. *Becoming an Effective Christian Counselor: A Practical Guide for Helping People* (Greenville, S.C.: Bob Jones University Press, 1996), 90.

50

obedience and serves as a mental exercise reminding the child of the parent's or teacher's original directive.

Though happiness is not the primary motivation that a parent should teach good doctrine and a child receive it (Proverbs 4:1-2), happiness is a wonderful consequence of receiving God's wisdom (Proverbs 3:13). Proverbs 3:17-18 states that the ways of wisdom are "pleasantness" and "peace, and "happy are all who hold her fast (NASB)." Though joy is more than merely an emotion (it is also a mindset; see James 1), the one who accepts wisdom dramatically enhances his or her life. Parents, however, who do not find their own life to be pleasant and joyful should not expect their children to pursue the parents' same values. With such a negative attitude of life, their highest value actually may not be God's wisdom.

Teach Right Motives and Desires (22)

An authority's instructions will no doubt go against the child's natural desire to want his own way, yet unseating his wrong desires is precisely what needs to be done; he must learn that life is not about getting his way or trusting his own heart. If a child is to live in order to please someone other than himself, there must be a change of heart, but this change will not occur naturally. Parents and teachers must teach the child that their instructions are more valuable than his deceptive desires and that their values benefit the child. The authority figure must also teach him to understand that future reward or benefit (represented as life and healing in verse 22) is worth the sacrifice of immediate gratification and getting his way.

Treasures and Pursuits

As with accepting God's wisdom, a child must also find greater value in his parents' or teachers' instructions and goals than in his own way of thinking. This discovery goes against his natural heart and thus directly affects his attention. Proverbs 4:22 states, "For [the father's words] are life to those who find them, and healing to all their flesh." Waltke states it as such: "The verb 'find' (gain, secure) is appropriate with *the command to pay attention* (20) [emphasis added], for that which is found is normally first sought (see 3:13)."[82] If the child, however, seeks

---

[82] Waltke, *1-15*, 297.

his own way instead of valuing his authority's directives, he will fail to carry through with those instructions.

The commentator Waltke notes of Proverbs that two metaphors are used often to denote the priceless value of divine wisdom: (1) a beautiful marriageable woman and (2) precious metal/treasure.[83] He states of the precious metals,

> [Silver's] intensifying, chiastic parallel, and *as for hidden treasures*, refers to objects so precious, such as silver and gold bricks or gems, that they need to be hidden in secrete places (Isa. 45:3; Jer. 41:8; Matt. 13:44) to protect them from thieves (4:7). The metaphor implies that a great deal of effort and sacrifice must be expended to get it (see 4:7).[84]

For the child to obtain such valuable wisdom will require both the child's and the parents' diligent effort and great sacrifice.

To whom or what a child gives his attention to reveals his treasures/pursuits and thus his heart—where one's treasure is, there his heart is also (Matthew 6:21). It can likewise be stated, where one's eyes (physically and spiritually) are focused there is his treasure/heart

---

[83] "When the object sought is a quality or an ideal, the goal is to fulfill a wish or realize a plan, and the verb takes on an emotional nuance" (Waltke, *1-15*, 222).

[84] Ibid.

(Matthew 6:22). Wisdom enables the believer to focus his attention on not only things of priceless value which he cannot physically see, but also on the future (2 Corinthians 4:18). Therefore, the child must learn to treasure others' wise directives more than his own desires. This lesson requires trust on his part and character on the part of his authority.[85] Parents and teachers should desire children to not merely obey and behave well, but to obey from an attentive heart, acting on right desires and motives. This is the same desire that the father in Proverbs had for his son. Longman writes:

> The father is not interested in just a superficial response from his son, some kind of behavior modification; he desires that his child be wise at his very core. Actions and speech will flow from a wise character. Verse 22 gives motivation to the son to pay attention to his father. If he takes the message to heart, then that will lead to life and wholeness.[86]

---

[85] Tripp writes, "If a child is going to honor his parents, it will be the result of two things: 1) The parent must train him to do so. 2) The parent must be honorable in his conduct and demeanor" (136). He also writes, "The primary context for parental instruction is set forth in Deuteronomy 6. It is the ordinary context of daily living. Your children see the power of life of faith as they see you living it. You do not need to be perfect; you simply need to be people of integrity who are living life in the rich, robust truth of the Word of God" (191).

[86] Longman, 154.

The highest motive for attention and obedience, must become the child's desire to please and glorify the Lord. This right motive, will propel each participant toward the finish line. The fact that motives are important to God — He will even judge man according to them (1 Corinthians 4:5) — is yet more reason to eliminate behaviorism as a viable solution for Christians to deal with a child's behaviors. A child's motives and desires are central to his ability to choose rightly and must be a parent's focus.

For biblical education to occur and the child to pay attention rightly, the parents must teach and promote right desires/treasure and motivation for the child, and eventually, the child should accept the parents' value system whole heartedly. If a child is taught only to conform outwardly to his parents' commands, then when he is grown and away from his parents' authority, his heart's desire will be unrestricted — what he truly treasures will be revealed. This truth requires that parents establish the highest value system based on divine wisdom for their child: what pleases God rather than self, church, or even parents' opinions. The philosopher Kant states,

> We must see that the child does right on account of his own 'maxims,' and not merely from habit; and not only that he does right, but that he does it because it is right. For the whole moral value of actions consists in 'maxims' concerning the good.[87]

A child's obedience to even a simple command, such as cleaning his room or remaining in his seat, must eventually come from a heart that values pleasing God above all else. Ultimately, paying attention is a matter of pleasing God.

In regards to ADHD, even secularists acknowledge that when a child diagnosed with ADHD likes something or finds something interesting, his bad behavior is minimal or even non-existent:

> Signs of the disorder may be minimal or absent when the person is receiving frequent rewards for appropriate behavior, is under close supervision, *is in a novel setting, is engaged in especially interesting activities* [emphasis added], is in a one-to-one situation (e.g., the clinician's office).[88]

The *DSM* also suggests as one criterion of alleged ADHD that the child "often *avoids, dislikes,* or is *reluctant* [emphasis added] to engage in tasks that require sustained mental effort (such as schoolwork or

---

[87] Kant, 77.

[88] *DSM*, 86-87.

homework)."[89] This reality reveals that part of the child's problem is misplaced desires. To remedy his natural propensity, parents and teachers must teach him right values that oppose his desire to please himself and to do only what he wants.

It is human nature to pursue what is most valuable. In many ways, life is a big treasure hunt and parents have the privilege/responsibility to first establish the premier value in the child's life. In the first eight chapters of Proverbs, both the father and Lady wisdom herself constantly admonish and call out to the son to find the highest value in life to be wisdom (Christ); a theme repeated throughout the first half of Proverbs. The father even admonishes his son to take Wisdom as his covenant bride and forsake those who falsely claim their worth when they in truth only devalue and destroy a young man's life. Paul sets forth the same truths in Colossians as he establishes Christ as the preeminent value and pursuit of life and warns of the deceptive/destructive nature of the flesh and world in which the believer lives.

---

[89] Ibid., 92.

57

Though Proverbs 4 primarily speaks in terms of moral instruction, the applications for parents' lesser directives to children are numerous. Children must be taught the highest value is to please God, and the acceptance of this understanding will motivate him to do all that his hand finds with his best effort (Colossians 3:23-24). The child who learns to value Christ and please Him, will consequently find value in giving his or her best effort in academics, sports, relationships, and chores around the house.

Not only must the appropriate treasures be clearly established, but desires which are wrong or counterproductive must also be laid aside. This step may require parents to disallow desired video games after school until the child's homework is done acceptably. It can also mean that the child forego activities with friends that encourage something other than God as most valuable (idolatry). The child may not like this repeated experience and may even make a scene, but learning to deny himself for something more valuable than his destructive desires is a lesson he must learn if he is to succeed in any endeavor.

Rewards and Consequences

Additionally, when parents give temporal instructions to their child, they should implement consequences for the child choosing right or wrong. Establishing consequences helps the child in many ways. For one, he learns that his own choices affect him and bring him and his parents either delight or sorrow. As the child learns to pay attention to his authority, he will realize value apart from his own way of thinking, and this understanding benefits him personally.[90] He also learns to sacrifice his desires for something greater and is taught self-control and patience necessary for a future focus and future rewards. These key terms are popular in secular theories of ADHD/ADD and are ideas which Scripture directly addresses.[91] In fact, the *DSM* even states, "Signs

---

[90] Waltke compares this verse to 1 Timothy 4:8, "Godliness has the promise of this life, and of that which is to come" (*1-15*, 297).

[91] "A disturbance in a child's ability to inhibit immediate reactions to the moment so as to use self-control with regard to time and future. . . . What is not developing properly in your child is the capacity to shift from focusing on the here and now to focusing on the future. When all a child focuses on is the moment, acting impulsively makes sense. From the child's perspective, it is always 'now.' But this can be disastrous when the child is expected to be developing a focus on what lies ahead and what needs to be done to meet the future effectively" (Russell A. Barkley, *Taking Charge of ADHD: A Complete Authoritative Guide for Parents.* rev. ed. [New York: Guilford, 2000], xi).

of the disorder may be minimal or absent when the person is receiving frequent rewards for appropriate behavior."[92] Though most secularists see rewards as temporarily and positively affecting the child's behavior,[93] they fail to agree with divine wisdom, which views rewards as a part of moral education to remedy the child's true problem.[94]

Though temporal rewards should never be the primary motive of obedience for a believing child, an obedient heart does bring about temporal rewards, and they reinforce the valuable lesson that self-control and self-denial bring future blessing. Ultimately, the child's receiving promised rewards should point his attention toward eternal life because Scripture repeatedly sets the reality of eternal punishment and eternal life as valid motivators for obedience.

---

[92] *DSM*, 86-87.

[93] Nancy E. O'Dell and Patricia A. Cook, *Stopping ADHD: A Unique and Proven Drug-Free Program for Treating ADHD Children and Adults* (New York: Avery Publishers, 2004), 38.

[94] Longman notes regarding Proverbs 3:2, that the child's first motivation to hear and to obey is the promise of a reward (131). See also Waltke, *1-15*, 104, 108-9.

It must be made clear though, that parents are called to reach the heart rather than to merely respond to a child's behavior with rewards and punishment. In fact, for parents to focus on behavior rather than on the child's heart will most likely encourage rather than address the natural foolishness resting in the child's heart. Authorities should give rewards and praise for wise decisions and consequences for poor choices, but they must also at the same time challenge the heart's motives and treasures. This necessity requires parents to biblically discipline rather than merely punish their children. The philosopher Kant remarks: "If you punish a child for being naughty, and reward him for being good, he will do right merely for the sake of the reward; and when he goes out into the world and finds that goodness is not always rewarded, nor wickedness always punished, he will grow into a man who only thinks about how he may get on in the world, and does right or wrong according as he finds either of advantage to himself."[95] In essence, when parents have a wrong focus, then the child's natural value system that seeks to please himself has only been strengthened by their

---

[95] Kant, 84.

61

approach. In contrast, notice the primary focus of the father's discipline in Proverbs 23:19. Before sharing with his son what he must not do (he does address the son's behavior), he calls him to attention and reiterates the son's responsibility over his heart's direction: "Hear, my son, and be wise, and direct your heart in the way." How a parent or teacher deals with a misbehaving child both shapes the child's thinking and reveals the authority's own treasure and motivation. Wise instructors focus on the heart and not merely on the behavior.

In order to have rewards and consequences, there must also be directives, rules, laws, and structure. These are necessary elements of helping participants to arrive at their goal and to be successful. Whether in a classroom or at home, authorities must establish rules and standards to eliminate chaos and assist in direction. Meeting a standard and following rules, however, must never be set forth as the primary goal. The law is merely a teacher (Galatians 4:24). Essentially, rules, standards, instructions, and principles guard the child's heart and help propel him toward the goal. In addition, rules must be crafted in accordance with the established goal. If a school's or family's rules and principles do not facilitate the established goal, then they should be eliminated. Biblical discipline is consumed with moving the participant from the character of a fool to the goal of the wise (Proverbs 1:2-4; 13:1), and God's discipline through grace provides the chief example (Titus 2:11-12; Heb 12:1-13).

Emphasize Personal Responsibility (23)

Additionally, parents must emphasize the personal responsibility of the child to hear, accept, and carry out their instructions. Proverbs 4:23 shows that ultimately the child will be responsible for his life's direction and outcome: "Keep your heart with all vigilance, for from it flow the springs of life." The child is personally responsible to keep or guard his own heart, which includes his behaviors (See illustration B).[96]

---

[96] Whybray, 82.

63

Though his parents guard his heart when he is young and teach him to do likewise, they will not always be with him to ensure this vital task is carried out. The prudent parent anticipates the child's future

Guard the Heart

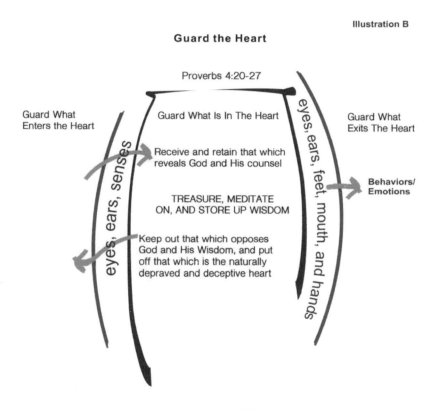

Proverbs 4:20-27

Guard What Enters the Heart

Guard What Is In The Heart

Guard What Exits The Heart

eyes, ears, senses

Receive and retain that which reveals God and His counsel

TREASURE, MEDITATE ON, AND STORE UP WISDOM

Keep out that which opposes God and His Wisdom, and put off that which is the naturally depraved and deceptive heart

eyes, ears, feet, mouth, and hands

Behaviors/ Emotions

Proverbs 25:28
"A man without self-control is like a city broken into and left without walls."

departure from his authority and disciples his child accordingly
(Proverbs 23:19). Simply stated, wise parents discipline their children
until self-discipline becomes a part of who the child is. This is not
discipline apart from regeneration,[97] but self-discipline for the purpose
of godliness (1 Tim 4:7-8):[98] "The task of education is to enable the youth
to raise his capabilities to the highest pitch of effectiveness and to set
him undeviatingly on the right road by disciplining his habits and
enlightening his attitudes."[99] The child must learn his responsibility to
diligently guard his heart, which is of the upmost importance and
directly related to his value system.[100] Doing so "must be reckoned as

---

[97] McKane, 564-65.

[98] MacArthur comments on this type of self-discipline, "**Discipline** is from *gumnazō*, from which our English words 'gymnasium' and 'gymnastics' derive. It means 'to train,' or 'to exercise.' The word speaks of the rigorous, strenuous, self-sacrificing training an athlete undergoes" (John F. MacArthur Jr., *1 Timothy*, MacArthur New Testament Commentary [Chicago: Moody, 1995], 163); see also Waltke's comments on 1 Timothy 4:7-8 (*1-15*, 297).

[99] McKane, 564-65.

[100] Whybray, 82.

more important than anything else that one needs to restrain."[101] One main objective of parents' discipline, then, must be to foster Spirit-controlled self-discipline,[102] which produces godliness and carries the child on *the way* beyond his days under his parents' authority. While children are young and immature, parents are called to give wisdom that helps to guard their children's hearts from those things which would destroy them and teach them to do likewise (Proverbs 2 provides some examples). The child that will not learn or lacks diligence apart from his authority's supervision is on his way to becoming a sluggard. The wise son, however, receives instruction to become like the proverbial ant. Again, biblical discipline is always centered on right goals, pursuits, and treasures that produce right change. In essence, biblical discipline is the parent's deliberate choice and consistent effort to point their child's attention toward that which they treasure most (Deut. 6:4-8).

---

[101] Waltke, *1-15*, 297. See also Whybray, 82.

[102] Kidner, *Proverbs*, 68.

Confront the natural heart (24)

At first glance, it may seem that Proverbs 4:24 speaks only of the

child's speech, however, the proverb also speaks of the natural condition

of the heart: "Put away from you crooked speech, and put devious talk

far from you." Obeying this command does entail controlling the mouth,

but because the mouth reveals the heart, reining in the tongue will

demand cultivating a heart that embraces truth and rejects falsehood.

"The mouth is given pride of place, for it is the direct conduit to and

from the heart. 'As one speaks, so is he.'"[103] The child's behaviors reveal

his heart and purpose, but his mouth is often the most revealing. Here, in

verse 22, the father addresses both the natural heart and its behaviors,

which are crooked (NAS: deceitful) and devious.[104]

---

[103] Waltke, *1-15*, 299.

[104] Those who plan to do evil are characterized by fraudulent or deceptive
hearts, which "is also the topic of 11:1; 12:5, 17, [20]" (Longman, 277). On Jeremiah 17:9,
Harrison writes, "Unregenerate human nature is in a desperate condition without divine
grace, described by the term *gravely ill* in verse 9 (RSV *desperately corrupt*, NEB *desperately
sick*). Cf. 15:18 and 30:12, where the meaning 'incurable' occurs. Every generation needs
regeneration of soul by the Spirit and grace of God (cf. John 3:5f.; Titus 3:5)" (R. K.
Harrison, *Jeremiah and Lamentations: An Introduction and Commentary*, vol. 21 of Tyndale Old
Testament Commentaries, ed. Donald J. Wiseman [Downers Grove: InterVarsity, 1973],
109). Craigie states, "From a human perspective it may seem that no one can know the

Many secularists admit that the natural bent of man is deceptive, yet they attribute man's deception to his physical brain.[105] Physicians Dr. Jeffrey Schwartz and Rebecca Gladding write about the importance of having what they define as "veto power" over the deceptive brain. They state that it is: "The ability to refuse to act on a deceptive brain message, uncomfortable sensation, or habitual response."[106] But Scripture concludes in passages such as Jeremiah 17:9 that "the heart is deceitful above all things and *desperately* [incurably] sick." Likewise, Proverbs 14:8 reads, "The wisdom of the prudent is to discern his way, but the folly of fools is deceiving." Man's spiritual nature, not merely his physical brain, are skilled at deceiving him, and God's wisdom is foundational to his restoration and remedy.

---

inscrutable heart of a person who is deliberately deceitful. [But] Yahweh is the one who searches the heart and tests the inward parts of humankind (cf. ובחנת לבי, Jer. 12:3). He knows the heart and gives to each according to the fruit of his/her deeds. This reference to fruit again links this passage with the preceding one (v 8)" (Peter C. Craigie, *Jeremiah 1–25*, vol. 26 of Word Biblical Commentary [Dallas: Word, 1998], 227–28).

[105] Jeffrey Schwartz and Rebecca Gladding, *You Are Not Your Brain: The 4-Step Solution for Changing Bad Habits, Ending Unhealthy Thinking, and Taking Control of Your Life* (New York: Penguin Group, 2012).

[106] Ibid., 35.

As previously noted, in order for a child to give his attention to someone else's desires and directives rather than his own, parents must confront the child's deceptive and sick heart.[107] In fact, Proverbs 12:15 describes a child's naturally deceptive way as: "The way of a fool is right in his own eyes,[108] but a wise man listens to advice." Notice in this verse the difference of attention for the fool and wise man. Longman notes of this verse, "The proverb is about remaining open to hearing the counsel of other people, which involves humility and the lack of pride."[109] The lust of the eyes, the lust of the flesh, and the pride of life summarize the child's natural position, which deceptively instructs him to think highly of himself and his own opinions, pursue his own values, and ignore the

---

[107] "The wise are not convinced that their way is invariably correct, so they are willing to pay attention to advice that they gather along the way" (Longman, 276).

[108] Longman states, "Unfortunately, the dupes [simple fools] are not sensitive enough to realize the problem with their lives" (275). Kidner also writes, "We show ourselves men of reason when we *listen* (RSV) to reason and test ourselves for prejudice. The person who always knows best may be the only one unconscious of his real name" (*Proverbs*, 97).

[109] Longman, 276.

69

counsel of others.[110] Proverbs 14:12 likewise states, "There is a way that seems right to a man, but its end is the way to death." One scholar translates the verse: "There is a path that is straight before a person, but in the end it is the path of death."[111] The child's natural way of thinking (the object of his attention) is to trust in his own way, and though to him it appears as the best and easiest way, it is actually the path to destruction.[112] Parents who confront the child's natural heart teach the child not to trust in his own way, but to place faith in the sound instructions and promises of others who love him. Such faith requires the child to listen to that which opposes his natural way of thinking (Romans 10:17).

---

[110] Waltke comments, "His lack of uprightness becomes obvious to others when he fails to exhibit self-control (16). His false self-evaluation is corrected by public evaluation. Moreover, it also introduces vv. 17-23, which pertain to speech, for although it does not pertain directly to speech, it is foundational to it. If one is wise (*hakam*) through listening to counsel (v. 15), he has the tongue of 'wise people' (*hakamim*) that brings healing (v. 8)" (*1-15*, 532).

[111] Longman, 300.

[112] Waltke, *1-15*, 591. "By metaphor of a 'journey' the proverb cautions youth against estimating on their own the consequences of their lifestyle. (see 12:15)" (ibid).

Because every child's heart is morally corrupt, each individual must have a complete change of heart. The depth of such change cannot be achieved by great striving on the parent's part: rather, it includes "a long deep process of unselfing."[113] The putting off of foolishness must first occur before a putting on or the renewing of the mind can take place. The child himself must confess his own deceptive and foolish nature. This process of change does not happen on its own: but "only by making [his] ear attentive (*lehaqsib . . . ozneka*; cf. 1:8; 1:24; 15:31) does [he] morally change."[114] Such a statement emphasizes again the idea that the child's repentance and thus his saving faith, in fact, will come from paying attention rightly. Parents must not only instruct their children in righteousness, but they must also reprove, rebuke, and correct their children's foolish nature (2 Timothy 3:15-17).[115]

---

[113] Iris Murdoch, *Metaphysics as a Guide to Morals* (New York: Penguin, 1993), 52-54); f. Waltke, *1-15*, 221

[114] Waltke, *1-15*, 221.

[115] Even the unsaved, when they give attention to the deception of their own hearts or listen to others who are foolish in nature are morally changing. Everyone is giving attention to someone or something, and no change, for better or for worse, exists apart

Proverbs 4:24 reveals the heart's natural state to be crooked and devious, but it also speaks of the behaviors and specifically the mouth to be likewise. The commentator Kidner states of this verse, "After the thoughts come the words (cf. Luke 6:45c; Romans 10:10)."[116] The reality that the mouth reveals the heart provides parents with feedback as to whether or not the child's heart is receiving their instructions and teachings rightly. For example, when children fail to carry out instructions, they sometimes make excuses for their failure to concentrate. Children sometimes offer the following as excuses for their disobedience: "I did not understand," "I did not remember," "I did not want to," "I did not know how to," "I felt as though I did not need to" (possibly no supervision or consequences), or "I was distracted." These excuses also make the parents aware of what aspect of attention the child must work on with more intensity.

from volitionally giving one's attention. It is also worth noting that the scorner in Proverbs is trying to gain the attention of the simpleton and lead him down a destructive path.

[116] Kidner, *Proverbs*, 68.

Essentially, the parent is able to draw out what is in the child's heart by what proceeds from his mouth.[117] For example, if the child states that he forgot his parent's instructions, then parents should redouble their efforts to repeat imperatives and establish expectations in the child's mind. He is struggling with hiding commands in his heart. If he seems as though he is not paying attention when parents are speaking directly to him,[118] they must with greater intensity gain control of his eyes, address any distractions, and confront any self-centered desires. If he repeatedly leaves his books and homework at school, parents must ask questions that allow his mouth to reveal his heart. For example, parents can find out what the child did directly after school and consider any distractions (e.g., friends, organized extra-curricular activities, or

---

[117] Proverbs 20:5 states, "The purpose in a man's heart is like deep water, but a man of understanding will draw it out." Kidner compares Proverbs 20:5 (ibid., 137) with Proverbs 18:4, "The words of a man's mouth are deep waters; the fountain of wisdom is a bubbling brook" (ibid., 128). Once again, the heart and the mouth are connected. It is not always easy for parents to understand what their child is thinking or saying, but divine wisdom makes it possible. Cohen explains parts of the verse this way: "*Counsel.* A person's real intentions as distinct from the words with which he conceals it. *draw it out.* His cultivated mind enables him to penetrate beneath the verbal surface" (132).

[118] *DSM*, 92.

personal hobbies) that he found more important than remembering his book bag. His habit also reveals that doing his best academically, a value his parents have established, is not as great a priority as other desires in his heart. Additionally, he must be given fitting consequences that will correct him and motivate him to value concentrating on this task. This necessity may mean that distractions (such as playing video games or sports) which impede success in academics (giving his best for the right reason) should be eliminated for a time. This process also assumes that parents have consulted with a physician to address any possible physical impairments of the child who regularly struggle with paying attention.

If children are only taught self-discipline, offered rewards, or encouraged for right behavior, yet the true nature of their hearts is never confronted, then they learn to pay attention in such a way that only facilitates their naturally foolish heart. In other words, they will listen and even behave according to expectations in order to get their own way. In truth, they are still giving attention to their own deceptive desires. Parents must, instead, rebuke, reprove, correct, apply appropriate consequences and instruct them in righteousness. Attention to the Word of God produces in the child the moral change that he desperately needs in order to be productive in this life in view of the life to come. This process of attention and change may be best understood as the child's need to learn to love God and others instead of himself.

STEP 3 – WARN OF BESETTING DISTRACTIONS (25-26)

With every task, goal, or directive, distractions abound, and they are not easy to overcome. In verses 25-26, the father admonishes the son: "Let your eyes look directly forward, and your gaze be straight before you. Ponder the path of your feet; then all your ways will be sure." The metaphor of the road is continued in verse 25, where the father admonishes his son to have single-mindedness in carrying out his instructions. In this proverb, the eyes and the feet must work together in order for the child to arrive at his destination. But the child must fix his attention: "When a man's gaze is fixed intently upon a goal his eyelids are naturally immovable."[119] It is key to again note step one: if parents do not teach their children to remain focused externally on their faces, then they should not expect the child to stay focused internally on set objectives. Staying focused with the eyes and the mind despite distractions is a skill that will help the child in the home as well as at

---

[119] Cohen, 25.

church and school [120] because "distraction is the enemy of all education"[121]; therefore,

> Distractions must never be allowed, least of all in school, for the result will be a certain propensity in that direction which might soon grow into a habit. Even the finest talents may be wasted when once a man is subject to distraction. Although children are inattentive at their games, they soon recall their attention.[122]

Self-control is essential for the child's success. However, the natural tendency of children is to be easily distracted: "The eyes ever search for new stimuli (27:20), and so the son must be admonished to keep them from straying to the wrong stimuli."[123] Proverbs 17:24 shows the foolish tendency to lose focus on that which is meaningful and significant and to give attention (through the eyes) to vanity.[124] The

---

[120] As is often the case in Proverbs, what is true in the physical world, illuminates what is true in the spiritual world. The eyes of the heart (desires/treasures) will determine the direction of the feet (life/behaviors).

[121] Kant, 73-74.

[122] Ibid.

[123] Waltke, 15-31, 300.

[124] Kidner, *Proverbs*, 126; Warren Wiersbe, *Be Skillful: Tapping God's Guidebook to Fulfillment* (Wheaton: Victor Books, 1995), 75.

verse reads, "The discerning sets his face toward wisdom, but the eyes of a fool are on the ends of the earth." So the fool is characterized by distraction and fantasy, whereas "wisdom is the focus of people with understanding, and that is why they have understanding. . . . [The fool's] focus is too broad and scattered."[125] This description explains why children labelled as having ADHD often choose to give their attention to things that interest them and not to their authority's instructions, and this description is also why the *DSM* states that the child diagnosed with ADHD "is often easily distracted by extraneous stimuli."[126] They are by nature simpletons without understanding or right focus, and as a result, they are easily distracted.

Children diagnosed with ADHD are characterized by not being able to think in terms of future consequences, so their distractibility, failure to complete tasks, and poor choices are often excused. Proverbs, however, sees both the wise child and the foolish child as having goals. The foolish child's goal is to please himself; therefore, he is often

---

[125] Longman, 350.

[126] *DSM*, 92.

impatient, impulsive, restless, slothful, and unsatisfied.[127] Furthermore, his desires can change at a moment's notice. Though the foolish have desired goals, they either plan to do evil according to their natural hearts,[128] or they fail to consider the future and thus fail to plan appropriately; they are either willingly headed toward destruction or blindly lost. Their evil plans, impulsivity, and hastiness destroy them and what they treasure (desires, dreams, wishes). "Chaos ever threatens to undo the created order, and, if unchecked by diligence, destroys hard-earned wealth (24:30-34)."[129] The wise, however, plans to achieve worthy goals that are measured or "bound by the law" (an unchangeable standard outside of himself)[130] and diligently pursues them.[131] The goal

---

127 Kidner, *Proverbs*, 42-43.

128 "Proverbs, though does not talk only about wise planning; it also contrasts it with foolish planning. God condemns such plans (6:18; 15:26). They are characterized as fraudulent (12:5b, 20a). Those who plan in such a way will not succeed but will wander aimlessly (14:22)" (Longman, 558).

129 Waltke, *1-15*, 455.

130 Longman suggests that Proverbs 29:18 shows that without the 'vision' or the law of God as central to goals, disorder ensues (557); Similarly, McKane sees the verse as meaning that "without a magistrate people are indisciplined [*sic*], but a guardian of the

of the wise, in contrast to the fool, is not based upon his own deceptive

desires but on external instructions and advice. This person plans out the

way to success after listening to the advice of others.[132]

Furthermore, planning is required in order to be successful.

Proverbs 4:26 commands the reader to "ponder the path of your feet";

ponder means a "succession of steps, by which vision is turned into

action, [which] demands practical planning . . . and the idea of weighing

up one's course of action."[133] Proverbs 21:5 states, "The plans of the

diligent lead surely to abundance, but everyone who is hasty comes only

to poverty."[134] In other words, this verse "goes on to compare those who

---

Law keeps it on the right course" (641). Again, children must learn that life is not about getting their own way; this truth is essential to their education.

[131] Waltke, *1-15*, 509. The wicked also plan, but their planning is motivated by evil desires (Kidner, *Proverbs*, 37).

[132] Steveson writes on the child's pondering: "He should think well upon the path that he takes in order that his ways should be established" (Peter Steveson, *Commentary on Proverbs* (Greenville, S.C.: Bob Jones University Press, 2001), 63).

[133] Kidner, *Proverbs*, 68.

[134] Longman, 557; Cohen, 138.

plan with those who are impulsive, and the latter end up with loss."[135] Teaching a child to plan ahead in order to achieve worthy goals (instead of allowing him to be lazy or hasty [Proverbs 12:20]) is crucial to giving attention because doing so will help the child to eliminate distractions, focus on the future, deal with his impulsivity, encourage self-control, and enable him to achieve success in the original directive.[136]

Scripture sees all children as naturally lacking the skills to set right goals and planning to achieve them, and it views the parents as responsible to teach these skills to their children rather than assume that the child will develop them.[137] This reality contradicts the widely accepted theory of ADHD proposed by Russell Barkley, the leading authority on the ADHD construct; His theory sees normal children as

---

[135] Longman, 557.

[136] Boice writes, "Eyes are needed for the study of God's Word. Here the author does not even speak of what the eyes should be turned toward, only what he wants them to be turned from; he wants to be delivered from "worthless things," or "vanities." Boice goes on to say, "If we are to advance in God's school, we must fix our eyes on the things of God, which are lasting, rather than the things of this world, which are passing away" (993).

[137] Unlike ants, who have no need of an overseer, children must be supervised and instructed (Kidner, *Proverbs*, 43). Additionally, much of Proverbs is parental instruction, which teaches the child how to live.

capable of developing the skill of pondering and the ADHD child as being incapable of developing a future focus and the self-control to achieve goals. Barkley states:

> A disturbance in a child's ability to inhibit immediate reactions to the moment so as to use self-control with regard to time and future. . . .What is not developing properly in your child is the capacity to shift from focusing on the here and now to focusing on the future. When all a child focuses on is the moment, acting impulsively makes sense. From the child's perspective, it is always "now." But this can be disastrous when the child is expected to be developing a focus on what lies ahead and what needs to be done to meet the future effectively.[138]

However, Barkley's statement describes not merely a segment of the population with ADHD symptoms but the universal temptation to act based only on the desires, emotions, and deceptive perceptions of the moment. Therefore, these children who are labelled can also be taught to act in view of the future. In fact, Proverbs 19:20 presents how focus on the future and ultimately future success are achieved:[139] it is by parents' offering counsel/warning and instruction/correction and by the child's

---

[138] *TCoA*, xi.

[139] Whybray, 284. Proverbs 19:20 reads, "Listen to advice and accept instruction, that you may gain wisdom in the future." McKane notes that this contrasts the "self-opinioned man" in Proverbs 16:25 (524).

82

paying close attention and adhering to their guidance. For a child to focus on the future, he must learn to establish goals and plan to achieve them: "Wise planning leads to *great confidence in the future* [emphasis added] such as that displayed by the 'noble woman' (Proverbs 31:25)."[140] Similarly, Kant notes this need: "If we wish to form the characters of children, it is of the greatest importance to point out to them a certain plan, and certain rules, in everything; and these must be strictly adhered to."[141] Contrary to Barkley's thinking, children do not merely develop a focus on the future; parents must diligently teach them to give their attention rightly. Such a reality explains why the father in Proverbs repeatedly sets his son's attention on the future consequences of his present focus of attention and decisions.

Parents will need to establish goals and structure apart from the child's natural desires and help to eliminate besetting distractions by proactively teaching their children to plan to succeed. This exercise can be done with the child's homework, personal projects, sports, and

---

[141] Kant, 85. Kant goes as far as to say, "Unmethodical men are not to be relied on; it is difficult to understand them, and to know how far we are to trust them" (ibid.).

household chores. For example, when faced with writing a book report, the child knows the date that the project is due, so he must, with his parents' help, plan out a schedule to both read the book and write the report. Parents should help the child write out all the tasks that need to be accomplished so that he can check them off when they are completed. Additionally, parents must help the child view these tasks as a priority and not engage in distracting activities before completing his daily task. This exercise can be done for a specific project or on a daily basis. Whatever this exercise is applied to ultimately reflects a treasure and the direction of the participant's life.

STEP 4 – SUPERVISE DILIGENTLY (27)

Because young children are not naturally like ants who are self-motivated to accomplish tasks without supervision,[142] parents must supervise and enforce their instructions if they want to teach their children to pay attention and rightly behave. Verse 27 reads, "Do not swerve to the right or to the left; turn your foot away from evil." The tone of verse implies the father's demand for "extreme separation from the wrong way and an extreme commitment to the right path. There is no third way."[143] The father is watching over his original command with yet another imperative that "demands" his son to obey. This reality is seen in the numerous imperatives given in this section. It should be obvious that parents cannot give a child instructions and then passively hope the child succeeds. Parents must, instead, actively watch over their

---

[142] Kidner, *Proverbs*, 43.

[143] Waltke, *1-15*, 301.

original directives.[144] Even the *DSM* acknowledges that supervision

minimizes or eliminates the observable behaviors that characterize a

child diagnosed with ADHD:

> Signs of the disorder may be minimal or absent when the
> person is receiving frequent rewards for appropriate behavior,
> *is under close supervision*, is in a novel setting, is engaged in
> especially interesting activities, *is in a one-to-one situation*
> [emphasis added] (e.g., the clinician's office).[145]

Once again Proverbs does not agree with the *DSM* that supervision is

somehow an exception to ADHD behaviors or only a temporary fix to

the child's problems. Instead, Scripture presents parental supervision as

an essential element in the child's education. It is imperative that parents

closely supervise the child and enforce the instructions they give. This

supervision must continue until the child is mature enough to wisely

engage his own heart in obedience and responsibility.[146] The father's call

to attention in verses 20-27 "underlines the idea that wisdom entails a

---

[144] Whybray notes that the passage (20-27) contains 5 admonitions (81). In other words, the father continues upon his original directive to make sure his son obeys.

[145] *DSM*, 86-87.

[146] The father in Proverbs is admonishing and supervising his son even when he is coming into maturity around the age of 20 (Waltke, *1-15*, 178).

lifetime of work and not a single decision."[147] One could say, parents must discipline their children toward the right goals until the child is mature enough and has cultivated his or her own self-discipline to continue down the same path with consistency and discernment. Self-discipline, then, toward the right goals, is a vital part of parents' instruction. Successfully taking a child to the point where he can walk alone down the right path is no easy or quick task; it will require patience and diligent effort, and there is no guarantee that he will choose the right way.

If parents and teachers have instructed children clearly, have made sure they understand the directive, and have established the plan to accomplish their desire, then they must consistently check that the children are working toward the set objective. Likewise, when the task is complete, authorities must inspect what they expect and follow through with appropriate encouragement or correction and fitting consequences. As parents and teachers repeat this pattern, the child learns to take his own initiative to establish, plan out, and accomplish important tasks.

---

[147] Longman, 154-55.

87

CONCLUSION

Proverbs 4:20-27 provides parents and teachers with steps to teach their children how to pay attention and by doing so become wise. This pattern of education is applicable to both seemingly unimportant, everyday learning situations and to the highest directives of divine instruction. Ultimately, this pattern of education encourages the child to give his attention first to his human authority and then to divine wisdom.

Furthermore, this pattern establishes as important what the *DSM* explains as activities that help minimalize or even eliminate a child's bad behaviors.[148] These *DSM* explanations and the criteria themselves are a partial testament to the wisdom of God's design and plan that parents diligently teach their children to pay attention rightly. In fact, the biblical pattern of paying attention found in Proverbs 4:20-27 directly addresses

---

[148] Secularists see these activities (such as close supervision or rewards) not as part of the solution, but as exceptions to the ADHD disorder.

eight of the nine *DSM* criteria of the ADHD label under *inattention*[149] and can remedy the remaining nine behaviors under *hyperactivity* and *impulsivity*. Furthermore, this pattern can be used in any setting where communication is vital: the home, school, work, or church.

Parents can shape the child's character by teaching him to pay attention, by overseeing what the child pays attention to, and by choosing what habits the child is allowed to repeat from a young age. Experience can bring some temporal wisdom, but if the child repeatedly practices foolishness according to his natural heart, he will only gain more foolishness; in other words, he will store it up for himself. Proverbs 14:18 warns the fool "that by habituation he is storing up only more and more foolishness, till, as in 24, it will be the only thing he has."[150] The simpleton or immature child receives "as a permanent possession the ignominy and shame of folly (*iwwelet*; see 14:17), a metonomy for the

---

[149] The exception is "often loses things necessary for tasks or activities" (*DSM*, 92), though a child's learning to pay attention rightly would also minimize the frequency of his losing valuable possessions. Thus one could argue that this criterion is also addressed, since the child, like everyone, would still lose things only once in a while instead of "often."

[150] Kidner, *Proverbs*, 109.

deeds and effects of intractable moral insolence."[151] In order to drive foolishness from the heart and lead children away from destructive habits, parents must repeatedly engage their immature child in God's wisdom and in wise behavior, patiently allow him to experience the sting of his foolish choices and the rewards of his wise decisions, and diligently teach him to give his attention rightly.

---

[151] Waltke, *1-15*, 596-97.

APPENDICES

APPENDIX A – THE UNION OF PARENT'S DISCIPLINE AND THE WORD

Throughout Proverbs the reader discovers the union of God's Word/counsel with biblical discipline. In Proverbs 1:8, the son is admonished to receive his father's *musar* (discipline) and forsake not his mother's *torah* (directives/purposes). Based on God's design of marriage, it is understood in the passage that the parents—through their covenant with each other—are unified and one flesh (Genesis 2:24; Mark 10:7-9; Ephesians 5:31). What may be easily overlooked in the same Proverb, however, is the union of discipline and the teachings (1:8). When parents enter into a covenant with the one true God, it is understood that they will direct their children to pursue this same passion (Deut. 6:3-7). Both of these words in Hebrew are directional; they intend to lead a child from being a fool to a wise man.[1] Proverbs 19:20-21 likewise states,

---

[1] In the Old Testament, "*Law* (*tôrâ*) basically means 'direction' or 'instruction'; it can be confined to a single command, or can extend, as here [Psalms 1:2 and Joshua 1:8], to Scripture as a whole." Derek Kidner, *Psalms 1–72: An Introduction and Commentary*, vol. 15 of Tyndale Old Testament Commentaries, ed. Donald J. Wiseman (Downers Grove: InterVarsity, 1973), 64.

92

"Listen to advice (counsel/purpose) and accept instruction (discipline), that you may gain wisdom in the future. Many are the plans in the mind of a man, but it is the purpose (or counsel) of the LORD that will stand." Counsel, advice, or warning, then should be understood as directing a child toward (or away from) a specific purpose and discipline/instructions the practical means to arrive at the established goal. Again, these are unified parts of the same thought. Parents aim to make wisdom the treasured possession of their child's heart, and their discipline includes warning, rebuking, reproving, correcting, spanking, illustrating, teaching, and exemplifying the desired direction (see illustration C).

In the New Testament the same union of discipline and counsel is again presented to parents. After establishing the union of marriage in chapter 5, Paul begins Ephesians chapter 6 by focusing first on the child's attention and obedience. He then states what parents must not do before he offers what they must do. Ephesians 6:4b says, "Fathers do not provoke your children to anger, but bring them up (*ektrapho*; mature them) in the discipline (*paideia*; instruction) and instruction

93

PARENTS' AIM

Illustration C

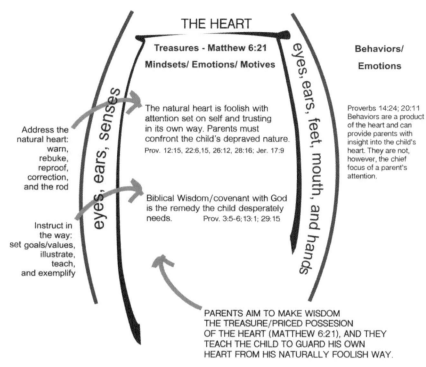

THE HEART

Treasures - Matthew 6:21

Mindsets/ Emotions/ Motives

Behaviors/
Emotions

The natural heart is foolish with
attention set on self and trusting
in its own way. Parents must
confront the child's depraved nature.
Prov. 12:15; 22:6,15; 26:12; 28:16; Jer. 17:9

Proverbs 14:24; 20:11
Behaviors are a product
of the heart and can
provide parents with
insight into the child's
heart. They are not,
however, the chief
focus of a parent's
attention.

Biblical Wisdom/covenant with God
is the remedy the child desperately
needs.   Prov. 3:5-6; 13:1; 29:15

Address the
natural heart:
warn,
rebuke,
reproof,
correction,
and the rod

Instruct in
the way:
set goals/values,
illustrate,
teach,
and exemplify

eyes, ears, senses

eyes, ears, feet, mouth, and hands

PARENTS AIM TO MAKE WISDOM
THE TREASURE/PRICED POSSESION
OF THE HEART (MATTHEW 6:21), AND THEY
TEACH THE CHILD TO GUARD HIS OWN
HEART FROM HIS NATURALLY FOOLISH WAY.

THIS AIM INCLUDES:

(1) Addressing the naturally deceptive/foolish
    nature of the child (putting off).
(2) Instructing him in the way that he must go
    (putting on Christ).

94

(*nouthesia*; counsel, purpose, or warnings) of the Lord. The parallelism of Proverbs 1:8 and 19:20-21 with Ephesians 6:4 is difficult to deny. The purposes of the Lord shall stand, therefore parents must teach their children God's way.

What is also significant about Proverbs 1:8 is the union between father and mother and the child's giving attention. Proverbs does not speak often about the mother, though she is mentioned. The Jewish way of thinking is that the husband and wife are one unit, and thus the father's repeated call for his son to give him his attention takes this truth into account—after all, it was established in 1:8. To damage the family structure, then, will most likely invite attentional problems to the child. It is of no surprise then, that research reveals this correlation: divorce directly affects young children's thinking and attention.

> The 10-year study revealed that the effects of divorce on children are often long lasting. Children are especially affected because divorce occurs within their formative years. What they see and experience during the failing marriage becomes a part of their view of themselves and of society.[2]

---

[2] American Academy of Pediatrics "Children of divorce: recent findings regarding long-term effects and recent studies of joint and sole custody." *Pediatrics in Review* 1990 Jan; 11 (7): 197-204.

Another study conducted for the *Journal of Abnormal Child Psychology* suggests that children with absent fathers (not due to death) are more likely to be diagnosed as having Antisocial Disorders, Conduct Disorders, and Attention Deficit Hyperactivity Disorder. The study further concluded that remarriage did not change a child's behavior.[3] When God's purpose and design for the family is altered or damaged, then this change directly affects the child's attentional habits.[4] This reality of course, does not dismiss the ability of God's grace to overcome the worst family situations, to allow a child to find his greatest treasure in the Lord, and to set his attention rightly.

In a similar manner, the union of discipline and the Word of the Lord directly affect the child's giving his attention rightly. Without the Word of God as the central aim of the parents' discipline and the child's attention, the child's life will reflect this deficiency. This reality is

---

[3] Pfiffner, L., McBurnett, K., Rathouz, P. (2001) Father Absence and Familial Antisocial Characteristics. *Journal of Abnormal Child Psychology.* v29 i5 357.

[4] This statement in no way implies that a child of divorced parents cannot pay attention or that he or his parents are second-rate citizens. It simply points out the reality that this unfortunate event in his life will affect him in every way.

precisely what Proverbs 29:18 states, "Where there is no prophetic vision [divine communication] the people [society] cast off restraint, but blessed is he who *keeps* [guards or treasures] the law [Torah]." If parents do not center the education of their child on the word of God, then unrestraint will be characteristic of that individual and his society, but happy is the one who treasures God's purposes instead of his own.

Also interesting to note is the covenant that Job made with his eyes, which he based upon what he should and should not give his attention to. He was to consider diligently God's wisdom, but not to consider diligently a woman that he was not in a covenant with. He bases his argument on his covenant relationship with God, since this is what he values and where he sets his attention (his greatest treasure). He also notes poetically that God's own eyes (his groomsmen) are diligently considering him. It is worth noting that Job even discusses the behaviors that were bound to occur if his object of desire and attention were wrong. Job 31:7 says, "if my step has turned aside from the way and my heart has gone after my eyes, and if any spot has stuck to my hands (behavior). . . ."

97

Giving attention rightly — instead of according to the natural man — ultimately comes down to a covenant relationship with God that values Him above all else in life. The parent's covenant with one another and with God should set forth an example for the child to follow. When parents have entered biblical covenants with God and one another, they will likewise make every effort to wed their discipline with the purposes of God and be able to call unto their children to do the same: "My son, give me your heart, and let your eyes observe my ways." (Proverbs 23:26).

APPENDIX B – THE IMPORTANCE OF THE EYES

1.   The eyes shape our hearts - Proverbs 4:20-21

"My son, be attentive to my words; incline your ear to my sayings. Let them not escape from your sight; keep them within your heart."

2.   The eyes can cause the heart to sin – Matthew 5:28-29

"But I say to you that everyone who looks at a woman with lustful intent has already committed adultery with her in his heart. If your right eye causes you to sin, tear it out and throw it away. For it is better that you lose one of your members than that your whole body be thrown into hell."

3.   The eyes reflect our relationships – 1 Peter 5:5b

"Clothe yourselves, all of you, with humility toward one another, for God opposes [*antitasso* – to look away from] the proud but gives grace to the humble [those whose spiritual eyes are on Christ]."

4.   The eyes can deceive our hearts – Job 31:1-7

"I have made a covenant with my eyes; how then could I gaze at a virgin? What would be my portion from God above and my heritage from the Almighty on high? Is not calamity for the unrighteous, and disaster for the workers of iniquity? Does not he see my ways and number all my steps? If I have walked with falsehood and my foot has hastened to deceit; (Let me be weighed in a just balance, and let God know my integrity!) if my step has turned aside from the way and my heart has gone after my eyes, and if any spot has stuck to my hands."

5.   **The eyes are never satisfied – Proverbs 27:20 and Ecclesiastes 1:8**

"Sheol and Abaddon are never satisfied, and never satisfied are the eyes of man."

"All things are full of weariness; a man cannot utter it; the eye is not satisfied with seeing, nor the ear filled with hearing."

6.   **The eyes reveal and determine our goals/treasures – Proverbs 3:21; Matthew 6:22-23**

"My son, do not lose sight of these – keep sound wisdom and discretion,"

**7.   The eyes (physical and spiritual) reflect our true character –
Matthew 6:22-23**

""The eye is the lamp of the body. So, if your eye is healthy, your whole
body will be full of light, but if your eye is bad, your whole body will be
full of darkness. If then the light in you is darkness, how great is the
darkness!"

8.   The eyes must be controlled – Job 31:1-7

"I have made a covenant with my eyes; how then could I gaze at a
virgin? What would be my portion from God above and my heritage
from the Almighty on high? Is not calamity for the unrighteous, and
disaster for the workers of iniquity? Does not he see my ways and
number all my steps? If I have walked with falsehood and my foot has
hastened to deceit; (Let me be weighed in a just balance, and let God
know my integrity!) if my step has turned aside from the way and my
heart has gone after my eyes, and if any spot has stuck to my hands."

SELECTED BIBLIOGRAPHY

Adams, Jay. *Back to the Blackboard: Design for a Biblical Christian School.* Phillipsburg, N.J.: Presbyterian and Reformed, 1982.

————. *The Christian Counselor's Commentary: Proverbs.* Woodruff, S.C.: Timeless Texts, 1997.

Alden, Robert L. *Proverbs: A Commentary on an Ancient Book of Timeless Advice.* Grand Rapids: Baker, 1983.

American Psychological Association. *Diagnostic Criteria from the DSM-IV-TR.* Washington, D.C.: American Psychiatric Association, 2000.

Atkison, David. *The Message of Proverbs.* Downers Grove: InterVarsity, 1996.

Barkley, Russell. "ADD, ODD, Emotional Impulsiveness, and Relationships." Available from http://www.youtube.com/watch?v=rcwp9T3zNcM&feature=related. Internet; accessed 4 March 2012.

————. *ADHD and the Nature of Self-Control.* New York: Guilford, 2005.

————. *Defiant Children: A Clinician's Manual for Assessment and Parent Training.* 2nd ed. New York: Guilford, 1997.

————. *Taking Charge of ADHD: A Complete, Authoritative Guide for Parents.* Rev. ed. New York: Guilford, 2000.

Barkley, Russell A., Kevin R. Murphy, and Mariellen Fischer. *ADHD in Adults: What the Science Says*. New York: Guilford, 2008.

Benedek, Elissa P. Review of *ADHD in Adults: What the Science Says*, by Russell A. Barkley, Kevin Murphy, and Mariellen Fischer. *Bulletin of the Menninger Clinic* 73, no. 1 (Winter 2009).

Breggin, Peter. "Medication Madness: The Role of Psychiatric Drugs in Cases of Violence, Suicide and Murder." Available from http://www.breggin.com/index.php? option=com_content&task=view&id=55&Itemid=79. Internet; accessed 12 July 2012.

————. *Toxic Psychiatry*. New York: St. Martin's Press, 1991.

Breggin, Peter, and Ginger Breggin. "The Hazards of Treating 'Attention-Deficit/Hyperactivity Disorder' with Methylphenidate (Ritalin)." *Journal of College Students Psychotherapy* 10, no. 2 (1995): 55-72.

Brown, Raymond Edward, Joseph A. Fitzmyer and Roland Edmund Murphy. *The Jerome Biblical Commentary*. Vol. 1. Englewood Cliffs, N.J.: Prentice-Hall, 1996.

Brownback, Paul. *The Danger of Self Love: Re-examining a Popular Myth*. Chicago: Moody, 1982.

Carey, William B. "What to Do about the ADHD Epidemic." *American Academy of Pediatrics: Developmental and Behavioral Pediatrics Newsletter* (Autumn 2003): 6-7. Available from http://www.ahrp.org/children/CareyADHD0603.php. Internet; accessed 3 May 2012.

Cohen, Abraham. *Proverbs*. London: Soncino Press, 1973.

Ellison, Katherine. "Brain Scans Link ADHD to Biological Flaw Tied to Motivation." Available from

http://www.washingtonpost.com/wpdyn/content/article/2009/09/21
/AR2009092103100.html. Internet; accessed 22 September 2010.

Elwell, Walter A., ed. *Baker Encyclopedia of the Bible*. 4 vols. Grand Rapids: Baker, 1997.

English Standard Version. Wheaton: Good News, 2001.

Fremont, Walter G., and Trudy Fremont. *Becoming an Effective Christian Counselor: A Practical Guide for Helping People*. Greenville, S.C.: Bob Jones University Press, 1996.

Hallowell, Edward M. "Dr. Hallowell's Response to NY Times Piece 'Ritalin Gone Wrong.'" Available from http://www.drhallowell.com/blog/dr-hallowells-response-to-ny-times-piece-ritalin-gone-wrong/. Internet; accessed 10 August 2012.

Hallowell, Edward M., and John J. Ratey. *Delivered from Distraction: Getting the Most out of Life with Attention Deficit Disorder*. New York: Ballantine Books, 2005.

————. *Driven to Distraction: Recognizing and Coping with Attention Deficit Disorder from Childhood through Adulthood*. New York: Pantheon Books, 1994.

Harris, R. Laird, Gleason Archer Jr., and Bruce Waltke. *Theological Wordbook of the Old Testament*. Chicago: Moody, 2003.

Hubbard, D. A. *Proverbs*. Dallas: Word, 1989.

Kant, Immanuel. *On Education*. London: Kegan Paul, Trench, Trubner and Co., 1899.

Kidner, Derek. *Proverbs: An Introduction and Commentary*. Tyndale Old Testament Commentaries. Edited by Donald J. Wiseman. Downers Grove: InterVarsity, 1975.

Kidner, Derek. *Psalms 73–150: An Introduction and Commentary.* Vol. 16 of Tyndale Old Testament Commentaries. Edited by Donald J. Wiseman. Downers Grove: InterVarsity, 1975.

Longman III, Tremper. *Proverbs.* Baker Commentary on the Old Testament Wisdom and Psalms. Grand Rapids: Baker, 2006.

McCabe, Robert V. *Old Testament Studies: Interpreting Proverbs.* Available from http://www.oldtestamentstudies.org/my-papers/other-papers/wisdom-literature/interpreting-proverbs. Internet; accessed 20 April, 2013.

McKane, William. *Proverbs: A New Approach.* Philadelphia: Westminster, 1970.

Murphy, Roland. *Ecclesiastes.* Vol. 23A of Word Biblical Commentary. Dallas: Word, 1998.

———. *Proverbs.* Vol. 22 of Word Biblical Commentary. Dallas: Word, 1998.

Newheiser, Jim. *Opening Up Proverbs.* Leominster, England: Day One Publications, 2008.

Phillips, Dan. *God's Wisdom In Proverbs: Hearing God's Voice in Scripture.* The Woodlands, Tex.: Kress Biblical Resources, 2011.

Rief, Sandra F. *How to Reach and Teach ADD/ADHD Children: Practical Techniques, Strategies, and Interventions for Helping Children with Attention Problems and Hyperactivity.* West Nyack, N.Y.: Center for Applied Research in Education, 1993.

———. *The Treasury of David.* Vol 2. New York: Funk and Wagnalls, 1885.

Stein, Martin T. "When Preschool Children Have ADHD." Available from http://pediatrics.jwatch.org/cgi/content/full/2007/110/1. Internet; accessed 17 September 2010.

Steveson, Peter A. *A Commentary on Proverbs*. Greenville, S.C.: Bob Jones University Press, 2001.

Waltke, Bruce. *The Book of Proverbs: Chapters 1-15*. New International Commentary on the Old Testament. Edited by R. K. Harrison and Robert L. Hubbard Jr. Grand Rapids: Eerdmans, 2004.

————. *The Book of Proverbs: Chapters 15-30*. New International Commentary on the Old Testament. Edited by R. K. Harrison and Robert L. Hubbard Jr. Grand Rapids: Eerdmans, 2004.

————. "Does Proverbs Promise Too Much?" *Andrews University Seminary Studies* 34 (1996): 319-36.

Weiss, Gabrielle, and Lily Trokenberg Hectman. *Hyperactive Children Grown Up: ADHD in Children, Adolescents, and Adults*. 2nd ed. New York: Guilford, 1993.

Weiss, Robin. "Babies and TV." Available from http://pregnancy.about.com/od/yourbaby/a/babiesandtv.htm. Internet; accessed 11 August 2010.

Welch, Edward. *A.D.D. Wandering Minds and Wired Bodies*. Phillipsburg, N.J.: Presbyterian and Reformed, 1999.

Wender, Paul. *ADHD: Attention-Deficit Hyperactivity Disorder in Children, Adolescents, and Adults*. New York: Oxford University Press, 2000.

Wiersbe, Warren W. *Be Skillful: Tapping God's Guidebook to Fulfillment*. Wheaton: Victor Books, 1996.

Whybray, R. N. *Proverbs*. New Century Bible Commentary. Grand Rapids: Eerdmans, 1994.

————. *Proverbs of Solomon*. Translated and edited by Philip Schaff and Charles Aiken. Vol. 10 of *Lange's Commentary on the Holy Scriptures*. Edited by Philip Schaff. 1898; reprint, Grand Rapids: Zondervan, n.d.